HOOK AND LADDERS

LARRY SHAPIRO

MBI Publishing Company

First published in 2002 by MBI Publishing
Company, Galtier Plaza, Suite 200, 380 Jackson Street,
St. Paul, MN 55101-3885 USA

MBI Publishing Company books are also available at
discounts in bulk quantity for industrial or sales-
promotional use. For details write to Special Sales
Manager at Motorbooks International Wholesalers &
Distributors, Galtier Plaza, Suite 200, 380 Jackson Street,
St. Paul, MN 55101-3885 USA.

Library of Congress Cataloging-in-Publication Data
Available
ISBN 0-7603-1141-2

On the front cover: Several elevated master streams were
put to work at this greater-alarm fire in Philadelphia in
November 2000. The truck pictured here is a 100-foot
Seagrave tractor-drawn aerial (TDA).

On the title page: This new, 100-foot, tractor-drawn,
Pirsch Senior aerial from Cincinnati takes part in a Fire
Prevention Week parade in Chicago in October 1982.

On the frontispiece: This is one of three 100-foot
Seagrave tractor-drawn aerials delivered to the FDNY in
2000, with shop number SL00003. It was assigned to
Ladder 6 in Chinatown. On September 11, 2001, when
terrorists flew commercial jetliners into the World Trade
Center towers in Lower Manhattan, Ladder 6 was one of
the hundreds of emergency response companies due on
the alarms. The apparatus was destroyed, but the entire
crew survived the collapse of the buildings. *Photo courtesy of
John A. Calderone/Fire Apparatus Journal*

On the back cover: Seagrave delivered this 1977 100-foot
tractor-drawn aerial with the open roof, and it was
assigned to Task Force 102. Some years later, the LAFD
began fabricating roofs out of fiberglass and fitting them
onto the cabs.

Edited by Kris Palmer
Designed by LeAnn Kuhlmann

Printed in China

CONTENTS

ACKNOWLEDGMENTS 6

INTRODUCTION 7

Chapter One THE BEGINNINGS OF THE HOOK AND LADDER 9

Chapter Two THE PROGRESSION OF MODERN TILLERS 23

Chapter Three DESIGN AND COMPONENTS 55

Chapter Four TILLERS IN ACTION 77

INDEX 95

ACKNOWLEDGMENTS

Writing this book on the heels of completing *Aerial Fire Trucks*, also from MBI Publishing Company, has been both challenging and rewarding. Challenging, because of the similar topics—both books on aerials—and the need to set these books sufficiently apart from one another. By their very nature, there will be some overlap, because the factual data about the progression of these aerials is integral to both titles. At the same time, it was rewarding because the second title gave me the opportunity to include additional information and images that did not fit within the physical guidelines of *Aerial Fire Trucks*. Because that title covers a vast number of trucks of many types, space for showing additional styles of tractor-drawn units that are included here was limited. As always, I am thankful for the opportunity to share these images and this information with others. I am also grateful for those images in this book that were taken by John A. Calderone, Joel Gebet, Warren Redick, and my sister Barbara, supplementing my own images.

When I began to research this topic, I was prepared to illustrate a decline in tiller use throughout the country. To my surprise, a great number of departments continue to use tractor-drawn aerials in front-line service, and some departments are even replacing other types of straight-frame units with tillers. This discovery led me to add something to this book that I had not originally envisioned. Chapter 4 includes what I believe to be a comprehensive list of fire departments throughout the country that are using tillers today. Unfortunately, it is not possible to guarantee the list to be all-encompassing, as there are no doubt some departments that have been omitted. I have searched through several resources and contacted many in a position to offer assistance in an attempt to compile the most accurate list possible.

I would like to extend my sincere thanks to the following individuals and groups who provided information and assistance without which this book would be highly inaccurate and boring. Jack Bailey, KME Fire Apparatus; Captain Garry Bradford, San Francisco Fire Department; Michael Braun, supervisor of the San Francisco Fire Department Repair Shop; John A. Calderone, *Fire Apparatus Journal*; Chief Michael Chandler, University of California Fire Department at Davis; Harry Close, East Penn Fire & Emergency, formerly with Hahn Motors; Jack Connors; Eli Ebersol, American LaFrance; Curt Elie; Earl Everhart, VTEC; Tom Finley, Philadelphia Fire Department; Chief Dave Frazeur, Los Angeles City Fire Department; Fire Chief William Graham and the San Bruno Fire Department; Rob Haldeman, American LaFrance; Dan Herb, the Sutphen Corporation; Chief Donald Heinbuch, Baltimore City Fire Department; Randy Hummer, American LaFrance; Ken Lenz, HME Trucks; Fire Chief Leo F. Leon, Watsonville, California; Jack Lerch, FDNY Fire Academy, honorary chief of department; Los Angeles City Fire Department, Task Force 26 and Task Force 27; Tony Mastrobattista, American LaFrance; Bob Milnes, Firefighting Innovations; Glen Prezembel, Mid-America Truck and Equipment Company; Steve Redick; Harvey Roth, FWD Seagrave; Lori Rausch, East Penn Fire & Emergency; San Francisco Fire Department, Engine Company 5 and Truck Company 5; Brian Smith, Baltimore County Fire Department, Eastview, Truck 15; the University of California Fire Department at Davis, A Shift; and the 2 Matts, Watsonville, California, Fire Department.

In undertaking this project, I risked invoking the wrath of my wife Dorothy who reads and edits the books that I write before they head off to the publisher. Being as supportive as always, she was behind me all the way with encouragement.

Thank you Dorothy.

INTRODUCTION

The terms "hook and ladder," "tiller," and "tractor-drawn aerial" evoke images at the very heart of the fire service. Their history can be traced back to the late 1700s, when horse-drawn steamers raced through the streets to fire emergencies. That excitement continued with the dawn of motorized equipment, which had to negotiate the same tight streets as their horse-drawn predecessors. The rear-steering hook and ladder, born of that challenge, has evolved into one of the most modern pieces of fire apparatus, while at the same time has remained one of its most traditional. This book will dispel some common misperceptions about the meaning of the term "hook and ladder" and will describe its origin and journey to modern-day firefighting. It has become evident while writing this book that the tractor-drawn hook and ladder is here to stay.

While monitoring the handline and elevated master stream, the UC Davis pump operator keeps a watchful eye on the gauges. Modern apparatus have color-coded gauges corresponding to the intake and discharge ports around the vehicle. Looking up the ladder, the fire department stores a roof ladder behind the sign plate along the base section.

The Chicago Fire Department purchased three of these Pirsch tillers with wooden aerial ladders in 1944. They were 85 feet long and used a spring-hoist mechanism. The two-section ladder produced a very long overhang extending past the trailer body. The enclosed cabs did not have any rooftop warning lights, just the bumper-mounted and grille-mounted colored lights. Firefighters rode on the running board along the side of the trailer holding onto the unpainted grab rail. This unit was assigned as Hook & Ladder 31. *Photo courtesy of Warren Redick*

Chapter One

THE BEGINNINGS OF THE HOOK AND LADDER

Pre-1900

It is possible that the first hook and ladder company in the United States can be traced to Philadelphia, Pennsylvania, in the late 1700s. This company's apparatus was not an aerial device, but a wagon, which carried several ladders and hooks. As building heights grew, the ladders became essential for access to the upper floors at a fire scene. The hooks, affixed to poles of various lengths, were used to pull down walls and ceilings to prevent the fire from spreading. As the length of the ladders grew, so did the size of the wagon to carry them. Rear wheels that could be steered were eventually added to improve the vehicle's turning radius, along with a seat for the fireman doing the steering.

Initially, large teams of volunteer firefighters pulled these units as well as the pumpers and hose wagons. Not surprisingly, this heavy physical work fatigued the volunteers before they even began the job of putting out the blaze. By the 1850s, when some city fire departments became professional organizations with full-time personnel, they used horses to pull the hook and ladders, replacing the volunteers. One of the reasons for replacing hand-drawn units with horse-drawn units was the expense of having to pay the large number of firefighters that were necessary to pull the rigs. With each change and advancement

in the fire service, it seemed that additional concerns arose. Before horses pulled equipment, there was never a need to provide transportation for the firefighters, since they arrived pulling the rigs. After horses took over the heavy work, departments had to figure out how to get the rest of the men there—in a more suitable way than having them run after the horses. They devised long steps, called running boards, which they added along the sides of the hook and ladder units. Running boards gave the men a place to stand and hold on while en route. Firefighters assigned to the steam pumpers and hose

This interesting combination rig running as Hook & Ladder 17 in Chicago utilizes a 1942 Mack LF tractor that was a spare piece. The 1938 American LaFrance aerial ladder was mounted to a trailer, which was built by the Chicago Fire Department shops. It is possible that the trailer was originally part of a horse-drawn company, but no definite confirmation could be made. Sandwiched between the main aerial and the long ground ladder on the side is a life net for catching victims who had to jump from burning buildings. *Photo courtesy of Warren Redick*

In 1942, Chicago purchased just one Pirsch tractor-drawn aerial with an enclosed four-door cab. Assigned as Hook & Ladder Company 44, this unit had a three-section, 100-foot ladder with a swing-away tillerman's seat. Although the ladder was aluminum, Chicago had not yet made a decision to change the fleet to metal aerials, and still purchased wooden ladders after this time. A roof-mounted beacon was added to the roof along with a bell in front of the grille. *Photo courtesy of Warren Redick*

wagons did not have this luxury, since their rigs had no room for the addition of running boards.

Some of the ground ladders that were carried had lengths of up to 75 feet. These were dangerous to use and caused frequent injuries to firefighters because they had a tendency to slip. In 1868, Daniel D. Hayes, a mechanic with the San Francisco Fire Department, addressed this problem with a design that anchored the long ladder to the wagon bed. Raising the ladder was accomplished using a worm gear, and the tillerman's seat was placed below the aerial ladder. Although this idea did not catch on at the time, American LaFrance purchased the patent and began manufacturing what they called the Hayes Aerial in 1881. This design featured a turntable as the base for a

Two American LaFrance 500-Series TDAs were delivered to Chicago in 1942. Each featured a four-section, 100-foot ladder with a fixed position for the tillerman beyond the ladder sections. A firefighter's coat rests along the side running board where he rode to the scene. Just behind the hand-held pump can is a basement nozzle. The "S" shaped nozzle is meant to fit through a hole cut into the first floor of a building so that it can apply water to a fire below. This unit was assigned as Hook & Ladder 1. *Photo courtesy of Warren Redick*

wagon-mounted aerial device that proved both popular and safe. The mechanism featured the worm gear and a crank system to raise the ladder, which then required several men to effect rotation and extension. Peter Pirsch and Sons began selling a horse-drawn hook and ladder unit in 1890. The Hayes Aerial design was later copied and modified as a spring hoist, which became commonplace. Seagrave introduced a spring-hoist-assisted design for raising an aerial in 1902 and American LaFrance followed with a similar design in 1903.

The 1900s

Motorized vehicles emerged in the early 1900s, but fire departments were slow to embrace the new technology. They were reluctant to replace their beloved horses. Cost comparisons showing substantial savings in switching to motorized power proved an important incentive. Companies experimented with battery power, gasoline-powered internal combustion, and a combination gas and electric hybrid unit in which the gas engine delivered electric power that was channeled to each

In 1954, the Chicago Fire Department received twelve, 85-foot tractor-drawn aerials plus a spare tractor from FWD. The aerials had two-section, 85-foot wooden ladders and were manually raised. Hook & Ladder 26 is pictured here at the fire academy. *Photo courtesy of Warren Redick*

wheel. The combination gas and electric units proved to be very slow and thus were not popular. One major drawback to early mechanized vehicles was their slower response time compared to horses. In addition, early power plants were not always reliable. Manufacturers of the new technology had to be diligent to win this market.

In 1909, the International Motor Company sold the first motorized aerial apparatus—actually a tractor to pull a previously horse-drawn aerial.

Seagrave followed this almost immediately with its own version. In the early 1910s, many more gasoline-powered tractors emerged for use in new aerials and as replacement units for horse-drawn trailers. American LaFrance, Christie (the Front Drive Motor Company), and Seagrave offered two-wheel tractor conversions. American LaFrance also made four-wheel tractors, as did the International Motor Company, Seagrave, and the White Motor Company.

Next Page: This 1954 Pirsch tractor-drawn aerial served in Kenosha, Wisconsin, the hometown of the Pirsch factory. Not surprisingly, all of the Kenosha stations ran custom Pirsch apparatus. This unit has a 100-foot ladder with a swing-away tillerman's seat, and an enclosed, custom conventional Pirsch tractor. Along the base section of the ladder near the turntable is a length of large-diameter hose that will be stretched along the ladder and fitted with a large nozzle for elevated master-stream operations.

In 1916, Seagrave was building city service ladder trucks—units without a permanently mounted main aerial—with and without rear-steering tillers, depending on the length of the vehicle. During the same year, the Ahrens Fox Fire Engine Company built their first aerial ladder with a hoist that used compressed air. It was an 85-foot wooden ladder on a non-tillered chassis and was available with tillered aerials in the early 1920s. Another company selling tillers in the 1920s and 1930s was Hahn Motors of Hamburg, Pennsylvania. The Stutz Fire Engine Company built only one aerial device, an 85-foot tractor-drawn aerial (TDA) in 1925. Seagrave delivered two innovative 65-foot TDAs to Oklahoma City equipped with 600-gallon-per-minute pumps. Mack began to sell aerial ladder trucks in 1929, offering 65- and 75-foot units with mechanized aerial functions.

Until the 1930s, aerial ladders were made of wood and were either spring-hoisted or used compressed air. In 1931, the Pirsch Company built the first fully powered wooden aerial ladder that could be operated by one man. Also during the 1930s, Ahrens Fox introduced a wooden aerial ladder with a nozzle at the end, combining the features of an aerial ladder with a water tower. American LaFrance, Mack, Pirsch, and Seagrave were still building wooden ladders in 1935, when Pirsch introduced the first aluminum three-section aerial ladder. This tractor-drawn ladder had a length of 100 feet and its operation was fully hydraulic. Pirsch continued selling a mechanically operated ladder series in 60- and 65-foot lengths, which were less expensive for fire departments. Seagrave offered an all-steel aerial—a three-section welded tubular steel ladder—in 1935. This non-tractor-drawn aerial was a hydraulic design with a reach of 65 feet. The heavier steel and aluminum ladders had to be raised and lowered with hydraulics; the spring hoist was not up to the task.

All aerials in the industry that offered 85 feet or 100 feet of reach were tractor-drawn through the late 1930s. In 1937, Pirsch redesigned their aluminum aerial with a new box design that they would continue to build well into the 1980s. American LaFrance began producing an all-hydraulic, four-section, steel aerial in 1938. Shortly thereafter, they were offering aerials of 85, 100, 125, and 150 feet. These tillered aerials featured a new position for the tillerman's seat. Previous three-section designs had the seat positioned over the rear of the ladder, which meant that the seat had to swing out of the way before the aerial could be raised at a fire scene. This new series placed the seat past the tip of the ladder in a stationary position.

In 1940, Ahrens Fox built their last aerials and began to concentrate on pumpers only. The following year, American LaFrance built a one-of-a-kind, five-section, 125-foot tractor-drawn aerial for the Boston Fire Department.

In 1950, American LaFrance produced their last wooden aerials with spring-assisted mechanisms. Pirsch was still offering both two-section wooden aerials and three-section aluminum aerials. Seagrave later introduced a four-section, steel aerial for their tractor-drawn units. Like the newer American LaFrance tillers, these four-section ladders had a

Opposite: Chicago Hook & Ladder 44, a 1942 100-foot Pirsch tiller with an aluminum ladder, is working at an extra-alarm fire on Chicago's South Side in 1959. As demonstrated here, proper deployment required the tractor and trailer to be jackknifed for stability. Something in this photo that is even more interesting, perhaps, is the unit working in the background. It is Chicago's very first Snorkel—dubbed "Quinn's Snorkel" after the fire commissioner. This unit was later fitted with a permanently mounted pipe along the boom sections to the basket. Visible is a 3-inch-diameter hose that is held in place with rope. This was not only Chicago's first Snorkel, but also *the* first elevated articulating platform used in the fire service. *Photo courtesy of Warren Redick*

Two Chicago tractor-drawn aerials are positioned to work at a 5-11 alarm fire at 55th and Normal Streets on the city's South Side in 1959. The closer unit is a 1954 Pirsch wooden aerial assigned to Hook & Ladder Company 20. The long rear overhang is clearly visible from this view. The aerial in front of the Pirsch is a 1956 FWD unit. Although it may appear so, the structure on the left is not burning. The fire is at a tire storage facility on the opposite side of the building. At the rear of the Pirsch unit is a basement nozzle, used by the fire department to fight basement fires after first cutting a hole in the floor above. *Photo courtesy of Warren Redick*

fixed seat for the tillerman that did not have to move for aerial operation. The end of the era for wooden aerial ladders came in 1955 when the FWD Company delivered 25 to New York City. During this same year, Ward LaFrance, like Mack, began to sell Maxim aerials. The B Model was then introduced by Mack and used for tractors to pull tillered Maxim aerials.

Throughout the life of the tractor-drawn wooden aerial ladders, fire departments used city service trucks and quads to fill the basic needs and duties of the hook and ladder. City service trucks were essentially aerial units minus the master aerial ladder. They carried ground ladders, hooks, and other tools that were carried on the tractor-drawn hook and ladders, but serviced departments or areas that did not require an aerial ladder. The other essential tools were still necessary at the scene of a fire and were not incorporated into the pumpers or hose wagons. Quads, which came about in the 1920s, were quadruple combination units that incorporated the city service truck with a pumper, hose wagon, and water or chemical-extinguishing agents to fill multiple needs for departments that did not need a larger

In 1959, FDNY took delivery of 11 tractor-drawn aerials with 85-foot Maxim ladders sold by Mack. The tractors had C85 Mack chassis and both the tiller and cabs had no roofs. The following year, an additional 13 identical aerials were delivered. In response to civil unrest in the city during the mid-1960s, the FDNY fabricated plywood roofs and partial enclosures for pumpers and aerials. Here, Ladder 121 is shown with the plywood modifications for both the tractor and tiller. *Photo courtesy of John A. Calderone/Fire Apparatus Journal*

aerial ladder. City service trucks were generally run by hook and ladder companies while quads were often run by engine companies or, less commonly, by hook and ladder companies. Seagrave delivered a quad to Hamtramck, Michigan, in 1956 that had a 1,000-gallon-per-minute pump and an 85-foot aerial ladder, but had no hose storage.

In 1959, Grove Manufacturing of Shady Grove, Pennsylvania, entered the aerial ladder market for the fire service, and within a few years they built just over a dozen units. One of their products was a four-section, 100-foot, steel aerial ladder with a tapered base section that could be mid-ship-mounted, rear-mounted, or tractor-drawn. Grove only built the ladder, torque box, and outriggers. These units were sold through Original Equipment Manufacturers (OEMs) that fabricated the trailers and supplied tractors. Several companies were aligned with Grove as OEMs.

The Hahn Company of Hamburg, Pennsylvania, was principally known for building pumpers, but in the late 1960s they were also an OEM selling

The FDNY received 10 replacement tractors in 1969 featuring Mack MB-series cabs. They used them to take the place of worn-out or damaged tractors while continuing to utilize the various trailers and ladders. Ladder 39 received one of these tractors, which pulled an 85-foot American LaFrance aerial purchased in 1948. *Photo courtesy of John A. Calderone/Fire Apparatus Journal*

aerial ladders, largely to customers who were already buying their custom pumpers. The first Hahn tillers featured Thibault ladders built in Canada. In 1963, Pirsch began to offer hydraulic jacks as an option for their aerials and Seagrave did the same beginning in 1964, although many customers still specified the manual jacks that were standard. Also in 1964, Pirsch began to offer the four-section, 100-foot Senior aerials and a fixed tillerman's seat.

In 1968, Grove built their first tiller, bound for Richmond, Virginia, with job number 210968.

Oren sold it with a Warner Swassey tractor. A second tiller sold by Hahn—job number 213169—the following year went to the District Heights Fire Company in Maryland. Between these two tillers, Grove built 21 straight-framed aerials, showing the comparative popularity of the two designs. Grove went on to build or sell four more tillers before selling their fire service ladder division to Ladder Towers, Inc. (LTI) in 1974. Of these other tillers, Howe sold one in 1971 to the fire department in West New York, New Jersey, with a job number of 217371; another went to Falls Church, Virginia, in

Here is a 1966 100-foot Seagrave tractor-drawn aerial from Torrance, California. The open-cab design was modified with a fiberglass roof to offer some protection to the firefighters from heavy rain. The three-section, 100-foot ladder required a swing-away seat for the tillerman. This unit was ordered with the optional hydraulic outriggers that were offered to customers beginning in 1964 to replace the manual jacks. Torrance, like several other California fire departments, preferred wooden ground ladders to aluminum.

1972 by Hahn with a Hahn tractor and job number 219972. A third tiller was ordered for Upper Darby, Pennsylvania, in 1973 and the last one was ordered for Charlotte, North Carolina, in the same year. Ward LaFrance sold the Charlotte and Upper Darby units that were assigned Grove job numbers of 732910 and 733010, respectively, and were in process at Grove when production was assumed by LTI; both units were subsequently completed and delivered by LTI.

The University of California facility in Davis (UC Davis) has a campus fire department with a full-time staff of 21 personnel, plus 15 student firefighters, who run a TDA, two pumpers, and a HAZMAT unit. Being close to Woodland, California, the home of Westates, a fire apparatus fabricator, they chose to replace their 33-year-old TDA using the local company. Westates was able to sell the Aerial Innovations aerial and paired it with a custom tractor by HME. The unit was designed as a quint with a pre-piped waterway and was built with one pair of H-style jacks. The quint concept allows the UC Davis Fire Department to deploy the unit immediately once on-scene to perform aerial rescues or to begin an attack on a fire. This unit has a 1,500-gallon-per-minute pump in addition to a 150-gallon water tank and a 50-gallon foam tank on the tractor.

Chapter Two

THE PROGRESSION OF MODERN TILLERS

The 1970s and 1980s

During the late 1960s and early 1970s, the four-section Seagrave tiller was very popular with fire departments. It used one set of screw-type jacks as standard and had an option for hydraulic A-frame jacks, which became standard in the mid-1970s. Regardless of the jack type, Seagrave recommended to operators that the unit be jackknifed for stability during deployment. American LaFrance, Pirsch, and Maxim, some of the other tiller builders at the time, also recommended that tillers be jackknifed. Only the LTI (formerly the Grove) tillers were meant to be deployed with the tractor and trailer in a straight line.

Throughout the 1970s and 1980s, the American LaFrance aerial product line included a tractor-drawn aerial with a 100-foot, four-section, steel ladder. There was no quint option or available pre-piped waterway, like those offered for the rear-mounted Ladder-Chief series aerials. Stabilization was achieved with four manually operated jacks—two per side—positioned amid-ship around the turntable with a 16-foot spread. Each jack was first pulled away from the body, and then the attached leg was turned toward the ground where it was gravity-fed after a pin was pulled. American LaFrance began to offer a hydraulic jack system for their aerials, including the tillers, in the early 1980s, though the tillers still required two sets of jacks. Both sets were A-frame in design, although each operated differently. The forward set was the primary stabilizer and had a swing-out design. Each was attached just below the front edge of the pedestal base and had to store horizontally above the rear tractor wheel like the manual predecessor. Once deployed, a hydraulic cylinder would push the jack out from the truck until it locked into position perpendicular to the frame. Then the leg would extend to the ground on an angle typical of an A-style jack. The second set was a radial arm design that rested straight up in the air. When it was deployed, the arm would arc away from the truck, following a straight path to the ground. This jack, like the previous

manual style, was attached on the running board at the forwardmost portion of the trailer.

LTI began manufacturing fire apparatus in 1974 when they purchased Grove Manufacturing's fire aerial ladder division. They offered a tiller as part of their product line from the beginning. LTI's 4S-100 series, which used a four-section, steel, 100-foot aerial ladder could be configured as a rear-mount, mid-mount, or TDA. Called the New Generation ladder, it had an optional waterway, a 200-pound tip load, breathing air to the tip, and tip controls for the ladder functions. The tractor-drawn version used one pair of out-and-down H-style stabilizers. When the New Generation aerial

As a means of saving money, some fire departments specify tractors that are adapted from commercially available trucks instead of ordering custom fire truck tractors for their tillered aerials. Aurora, Colorado, had Pirsch modify this GMC 9500 by adding a rear-facing bench seat with a canopy roof in addition to the fifth-wheel hookup. The truck was built in 1968 with a 100-foot Senior aerial and a fixed-tiller cab. Manual jacks are visible tucked under the turntable and the door to the tiller cab has the bubble window that was a popular option to protect the tillerman from severe weather. *Photo courtesy of Barbara Shapiro*

This 100-foot Maxim tractor-drawn aerial was delivered to Boston in 1973. Assigned here as Ladder 1, this unit had minimal storage compartments for equipment and utilized manual jacks for stability. The large silver handle on the side of the jack was used to pull it out before releasing the leg to meet the ground.

was originally introduced, the nozzle for a pre-piped waterway protruded past the tip of the fly section. To accommodate this, the fly section was extended past the nozzle in 1976, making the aerial length 104 feet, at which point it was designated an NG 4S-104. The end of the extended fly section had a squared-off design. These were also available with a tapered design or with custom-length fly sections to accommodate the overall length of the vehicle based on the requests of a fire department.

LTI also offered the Challenger series, which was an updated version of the original four-section

Grove ladder with the tapered base section. This ladder could also be configured as a tractor-drawn aerial. It was a lighter weight alternative to the New Generation.

Although LTI completed and delivered the last two tractor-drawn aerials sold by Grove, the first tiller sold under the LTI name was serial number 754013 for Talleyville, Delaware. This aerial was the first LTI tiller with the New Generation ladder. Previous units built or sold by Grove used the Challenger design. One other first for this unit was the use of a Mack CF series tractor. LTI's next tillers utilized the Challenger series ladder.

In 1973, Ward LaFrance sold two 100-foot tractor-drawn aerials with Challenger-style ladders by Grove. One, with Grove job number 732910, was to go to Upper Darby, Pennsylvania. A new company called Ladder Towers, Inc. (LTI) purchased the fire service aerial ladder division from Grove in 1974. Production for both of the Ward LaFrance units was transferred to LTI, who completed trucks. The unit pictured here from New Brunswick, New Jersey, was originally built for Upper Darby. It was bought by Ferndale, Maryland, when Upper Darby retired it and then purchased by New Brunswick in 1992. This is one of only a few units ever built with a custom Ward LaFrance Ambassador-series tractor. *Photo courtesy of Joel Gebet*

The first was an unusual unit with a Pemfab Wedge cab for the tractor and a body by Fire Trucks, Incorporated. The unit, with a job number of 770613, was sold to the U.S. Navy and deployed in Japan. Also in 1977, two tillers—job numbers 772513 and 772613—were ordered for Arlington, Virginia. Again, these used the Challenger series ladder and were pulled by custom Hahn tractors with Hahn bodywork.

Pirsch had a long history with fire service aerial ladders. The Pirsch all-aluminum aerials were in service throughout the country. They offered midship-mounted units, rear-mounts, and TDAs. These ladders featured all-riveted construction with 200-pound distributed load capacities. They had a "T" rail design that consisted of solid bottom rails with "U" shaped upright support rails. The ladder was extended with a drum winch pulling the cables. Due to the weight restraints, a pre-piped waterway was only available along the base section. The riveted design was instituted after George Layden, Pirsch's Chief Engineer in the 1930s, examined the riveted construction of the U.S. Steel building in Pittsburgh. He noted that the building was constructed to be flexible and carried this design into the ladders so that they too would be flexible and not break. Depending on the size of the ladder, it required one or two pairs of manual jacks or one set of hydraulic A-jacks for stabilization. The manual jacks, standard on aerials for many years, were a

Evanston, Illinois, among other things, is the home of Northwestern University. The fire department has utilized tractor-drawn aerials for many years, including this 1969 100-foot Pirsch Senior aerial. The tractor features a Pirsch custom safety cab that was fabricated by hand in their plant. The unique cab was much sought after, but was discontinued in 1981 because of the prohibitive cost to produce it. The Evanston aerial features a long three-section ladder with a swing-away seat for the tiller, lots of custom cabinetry, and manual stabilizer jacks. This unit was retired in 1991 and replaced with a new Pierce TDA.

screw-type design. This was a gravity-fed system that required the operator to swing or pull the jack out from the truck by hand. Then, after pulling a pin, the jack would corkscrew down of its own weight and stop when it hit the ground. The pin was then replaced to lock the jack into place. Upon completion, the jack was cranked up by hand before being swung or pushed back into a compartment. The hydraulic jacks for a non-tillered aerial were a radial A-configuration, and were stored in the up position along the side of the truck with the ground

pads at the top. For use, the jacks would fold down into place. Tractor-drawn aerials used conventional A-style jacks at the front of the tiller trailer. By the late 1970s, the hydraulic jacks became standard on all Pirsch aerials.

In the 1980s, Seagrave continued to build the Rear Admiral. This was a 100-foot, four-section, rear-mounted, aerial ladder on a single-axle chassis. The Rear Admiral was modified in the early 1980s to offer a heavier-duty ladder with a 200-pound tip load. This aerial required a tandem-axle chassis and had two rear-mounted, H-style outriggers. Called the HD100, it was also available as a TDA, which required replacing the standard A-style jacks with two swing-out jacks under the turntable.

In 1981, LTI made an exclusive agreement with Mack Trucks to provide them with an aerial product line. Mack then introduced the Bulldog I line of steel aerials. This was a completely new ladder designed to replace the LTI Challenger series. The Bulldog I, though, was only available to Mack. The Bulldog I series offered mid-ship ladders, rear-mounted ladders, and TDAs. These were four-section, 106-foot, steel aerials with a 200-pound tip load. They were primarily offered

on a single-axle CF611 chassis with a variety of engine options from 235 to 350 horsepower. The first tiller with serial number 8200103 (03 signified a Bulldog TDA) was sold to Downey, California. The Bulldog I aerials were offered with an optional pre-piped waterway. These came with an extended fly section to protect the nozzle and were measured to be 108 feet. Four of the pre-piped units were manufactured under the Bulldog series, but only one was a tractor-drawn unit, built on an MC chassis for Atlantic City, New Jersey. The Bulldog program did not prove to be very successful. A total of 25 aerials were sold before Mack ceased fire truck production in 1983. The Bulldog I was now

This 1974 100-foot, 1000-series American LaFrance TDA was assigned to San Francisco Truck 16. The abundant wooden ground ladders that are stored inside the body and outside were built in the fire department's ladder shop. This vintage aerial used two pair of manual jacks for stability. One can be seen resting horizontally underneath the turntable and the second is stored on the running board at the front of the trailer. The tiller cab is an early, rudimentary design with a hinged roof that was necessary to give the driver enough room to get into and out of the cab. *Photo courtesy of Barbara Shapiro*

In 1981, Hahn built the first tractor-drawn Fire Spire aerial ladder. Although many Fire Spire ladders were sold, only four were ever made as tillers. Two of the four were purchased by the District of Columbia Fire Department, one in 1981 and the other in 1982. The tiller cabs were built with plexiglass side windows in the sliding doors to provide optimal visibility for the tillerman. The hydraulic jacks used by Hahn were different from those offered by others. The upper portion of each leg was pushed out from the body before the lower section angled to the ground. The mechanical siren on one corner of the bumper and the traditional bell on the other corner supplemented the single-beacon warning device on the tractor roof. This unit was assigned to Truck 6.

available to replace the much heavier New Generation series as the primary LTI aerial ladder. The new designation became the Quadra Stix. The QS series, as it was generally called, included the QS-106, which was the 106-foot rear-mount, and the QS-106 TDA, which was tractor-drawn. The QS series had a 250-pound tip load, which was achieved with either a tandem-axle chassis or by replacing front downriggers with outriggers. When fitted with a waterway, the fly section was extended to protect the nozzle,

thereby lengthening the ladder. The designation then was a QS-108 or a QS-108 TDA. For a specific customer request, the fly section could be removed to create an 85-foot ladder.

By 1981, Hahn had entered the tiller market with the four-section, Fire Spire 106-foot ladder. Hahn only built four tillers, with two going to the District of Columbia Fire Department (DCFD) in 1981 and 1982. The other two tillers went to Waldorf, Maryland, in 1981 and Woodbridge, Virginia,

The District of Columbia Fire Department received this 100-foot, tractor-drawn Pirsch Senior aerial in 1978 with a tractor built by Sutphen. Assigned to Truck 11, this unit had manual jacks, an aluminum ladder at the rear of the trailer for access to the enclosed tiller cab, and was outfitted with fans, electric cord reels, and portable scene lighting. The rear section of the tractor had additional seating for firefighters. The low enclosure had no roof and the seating faced forward.

in 1982. The Fire Spire tiller used one pair of hydraulic outriggers, which worked differently from the A-frame jack common at the time. The jackleg had two parts—a vertical cylinder and a foot that was horizontal when stored. When the jack was deployed, the vertical cylinder would push the lower portion away from the body, where it would then angle down to the ground. In addition to the

four tillers they built, Hahn also provided custom tractors for one Pirsch tiller and for an LTI tiller purchased in 1981 by the DCFD.

In 1983, Pirsch unveiled a new aerial ladder design. The Skytop, as it was called, was a four-section, 110-foot aluminum ladder with a 200-pound tip load. This new design incorporated several changes from the earlier ladder, which was still available after

In 1981, the Baltimore City Fire Department took delivery of a tractor-drawn 100-foot Senior aerial from Pirsch. Kenosha, Wisconsin, the hometown of the Pirsch factory, received a similar ladder. Being a custom builder, Pirsch tailored each delivery to meet the needs and requests of the purchasing fire department. Although these aerials have the same aluminum ladder and Cincinnati cab, they have many differences. First, the body designs for equipment storage on the trailers are very different, with Kenosha using compartments of the same height along the entire length of the trailer. Baltimore designed different-sized compartments in front of and behind the wheel well that do not run the full length, leaving open transverse space for long tools. Kenosha ordered the standard, manual stabilizer jacks tucked under the turntable and an open tiller seat for the tillerman. Baltimore upgraded to the A-style hydraulic jacks as well as a fully enclosed tiller cab with sliding doors.

the release of the Skytop. Changes included a pre-piped waterway option along the entire ladder, "K" bracing, hydraulic cylinders pulling the extension cables, and nylatron pads replacing rollers between the ladder sections. The Skytop also used one pair of H-style stabilizers. The construction differed from the previous design in the use of welded bottom rails and ladder rungs that were made of hollow, tubular aluminum extrusions instead of the "T" rails. The uprights and the top rails were still riveted, a long-standing characteristic of Pirsch aerials. These changes enabled Pirsch to increase the capacity and add 10 feet to the length. Although the Skytop and the earlier Pirsch ladder designs shared the 200-pound rating, the stability and use of the new ladder was greater than the original design. The Skytop had greater maneuverability and was rated to operate at low angles, unlike the previous design. Greater range of operation was particularly important to Pirsch's ability to compete with other aerial builders and keep up with the demands of the fire service. The original aerial ladders, like so many that originated in the 1930s, were no more than long, powered ground ladders. These were intended to increase the height that could be reached with a ladder raised by men, and at the same time add the ability to turn for better positioning. Early aerial ladder designs were meant to be rested against a building during ladder operations. They were not built for cantilevered support. When the fire service wanted to add water tower abilities, increase load capacity, and provide rescue capabilities unsupported by a building, the early designs were not up to the tasks. Some early ladders built by other companies had a base section that was not as strong as the mid-section. This was fine when the ladder was used as intended (resting against a building). The Skytop was offered as a rear-mount or a TDA. Only three 110-foot Skytop TDAs were ever built. One went to Little Rock, Arkansas; one was delivered to a fire department in Tennessee; and the third was one of two TDAs ever sold to the U.S. Navy.

Steeldraulics was a small company that split away from LTI to build ladders on their own. They began with an aerial platform design that was eventually purchased and manufactured by Grumman. After that happened in 1983, they moved and continued as a company that primarily refurbished fire apparatus, but they also built four steel aerial ladders. All of these made their way to the San Francisco Fire Department. Two were 75-foot quints, delivered in 1985, and the other two were 100-foot TDAs, delivered in 1986. Because of controversy between the fire department, the firefighter's union, and the city, the 75-foot quints were sold by the city and never went into service in San Francisco. The TDAs were assigned to city ladder companies, and one is still on the roster as a reserve unit.

In 1985, after shutting down in 1980, Maxim re-opened under new ownership. They offered pumpers and aerials with the cab forward F series and the conventional S series. A Canadian company purchased 50 percent of Maxim in 1987 and then the other 50 percent in 1988 in order to infuse more capital. During 1989, Maxim was building about one truck per week. One of the last aerials produced was a tractor-drawn unit for Cambridge, Massachusetts. Maxim closed for the last time in December 1989.

By 1986, the 100-foot American LaFrance TDA, now called a Ladder-Chief, was offered with new features and options. Hydraulic jacks became standard, along with an enclosed tillerman's cab. When an optional pre-piped waterway was added it changed the designation to a TDA Water-Chief.

Seagrave unveiled the 550-pound RA110 ladder in 1987. This had a length of 110 feet and was offered as a rear-mount or tractor-drawn aerial. This heavier tiller required additional stabilizers. Seagrave installed two sets of swing-out "butterfly" jacks. Two jacks on each side were stored under the turntable with the larger, forward-sitting jack hinged just above the tractor's rear axle. The second jack, which was hinged slightly further back but still under the turntable, tucked in behind the forward leg.

The career Baltimore County firefighters assigned to Station 15 in Eastview, Maryland, used this American LaFrance 100-foot aerial between 1983 and 1995. This unit was ordered with a fully enclosed four-door Century Series cab and heavy-duty ladder. The hydraulic jacks replaced the manual jacks and were similar to those used on other American LaFrance aerials, but the front set required modification so that there was a place to store them under the turntable. Unlike the rear set of jacks, which rested in a vertical position, the front set had to lay down on their sides, necessitating a pivot movement to swing them out before they could be deployed down to the ground in a conventional A-style design. The tiller cab was now a full structure with a permanent roof and sliding doors.

These jacks were pushed out individually with hydraulic cylinders to their preset positions. When deployed, the forward jack was at an angle slightly greater than 90 degrees to the body and the rear jack was at an angle less than 90 degrees. Once set in place, each had an extension that went to the ground. Less than a dozen of the RA110 tillers were built.

In 1988, LTI introduced the QH-110. This was the Quadra Heavy aerial with a 500-pound tip load, wet or dry. It was another totally new design with wider rung rails than the QS series. The QH had heavier lift cylinders, higher handrails, and a heavier turntable, and was also offered with an optional waterway. This was available as a rear-mount or

33

The FDNY has always used tillered aerial apparatus, although there has been a steady decline in the number of tractor-drawn units since the early 1960s, when rear-mounts and tower ladders began to enter service. Ladder 40 received this Seagrave 100-foot TDA in 1980. The middle window of the fully enclosed P-series cab was removed in the hot summer months to give firefighters relief from both the weather and the heat from the motor, which was in the back of the cab. Common to FDNY companies is some manner of making their rigs unique as evidenced here by the slogan "Life Begins at 40." This tiller has added storage compartments on the tractor behind the cab, but is not outfitted with an abundance of storage compartments on the trailer.

TDA. Viewed by some as being too long, the 110-foot tractor-drawn was shortened and offered as a 100-foot QH-100. Initially, the TDAs required swing-out stabilizer jacks that extended in an arc to the set position. The spread was 18 feet and there was no option for short-jacking the outriggers. Deployment required a lot of room for the jacks to swing outward and away from the trailer. When there was not enough room for the outriggers, the trailer could be jackknifed to offset the opposite side outrigger. In the mid-1990s, the swing-out design was replaced with two sets of traditional outriggers with the same 18-foot spread, allowing easier deployment and requiring less space on the fire ground for setup. Atlanta was one of the last customers to purchase the swing-out jacks. Sixty-four

In 1983 when this aerial was built, Pirsch was offering the 100-foot Senior aerial pictured here as well as their new 110-foot Skytop aerial design introduced the same year. Ocean City, New Jersey, took delivery of this unit after it was displayed at the New York State Chiefs Show that summer. The tractor features a Cincinnati cab that became Pirsch's custom cab offering in 1981, when they decided building their own cab was cost-prohibitive. Since this photo was taken prior to delivery, the entire bottom section of the trailer under the ground ladders is open with no equipment mounted. This allows a view of the full width space that was available for placement of hand tools and fans.

QH-110 units were produced through 1996. The last unit was a tractor-drawn with a tandem-axle tractor produced for Columbus, Ohio, with a serial number of 9604509.

Also in 1988, Pierce entered the tractor-drawn aerial market with a four-section, 105-foot ladder built by Smeal, exclusively for Pierce. The TDA had a 400-pound tip load and used two swing-out, H-style outriggers with an 18-foot spread. The original tractor featured a modified Dash cab with a raised roof panel that allowed the tillerman to see the cab. Pierce also had a turntable leveling system capable of adjusting to a 10-degree front-to-back angle and to 4 degrees from side to side. The turntable was hinged to the trailer, which allowed the pedestal to be leveled with the horizon regardless of the trailer

Preceding pages and below: Seagrave built both of these 100-foot tractor-drawn aerials in 1983. The cabs are the same and the compartments on the tractors are similar. The different trailer bodies illustrate how easy it is to customize these units to match fire department specifications. In addition, although each has an enclosed tiller cab, they are completely different. The San Francisco tiller has a rudimentary enclosure with no doors and a simple roof with a flap that folds open to allow the driver to stand up. Tillermen rarely ever closed the flap, unless it was raining very heavily. The Fairfax County tiller, which was assigned as Truck 8 in Annandale, Virginia, has a full enclosure for the tillerman albeit a small one. The Fairfax unit has a buddy seat outside the tiller cab for training and was ordered with the available hydraulic A-style jacks, whereas Truck 12 from San Francisco has the standard manual jacks. One other difference between the two TDAs is the exterior mounting of additional ground ladders in San Francisco, which reflects their practice of using lots of ladders.

In 1993, the fire department in Niles, Illinois, replaced their 1970 Pirsch TDA with a new 105-foot Pierce tiller. This was the last tractor-drawn aerial sold by Pierce that featured a Smeal ladder. Although Pierce and Smeal dissolved their relationship in 1991, many aerial orders that were in process at the time were completed in the year or so following. Niles ordered this tractor with a tandem rear axle, which they found necessary to achieve a 500-pound-rated tip load. The bedded ladder position, which comes to the roof of the tiller cab, is higher than most tillers and presented visibility problems for the tillerman. Subsequently, the light bar on the front of the cab was mounted on tall brackets to give the tillerman sight of the truck cab. To increase the tillerman's downward visibility, the department mounted no ladders or other equipment above the low compartments, with the exception of a single positive pressure fan. This design utilizes swing-out-style hydraulic jacks.

position. The mechanism to implement this leveling inherently raised the turntable, which was one factor in raising the entire ladder when it was stored. This higher position placed the handrails of the bedded ladder above the cab of the tractor, causing the need for the raised roof panel on the tractor. This design severely hampered the tillerman by limiting visibility from the rear cab. The tiller cab was large, capable of accommodating two people. The Pittsburgh Fire Department purchased the first several tillers with the leveling system but subsequently took them out of service and sold them to other departments.

The Sutphen Company is probably best known for their mid-mount towers with box-boom construction. In the early 1990s, they introduced a new ladder with a three-sided design and offered it as a mid-mount on a straight frame and later as a tractor-drawn aerial. Only three of the TDAs have been built, the last of which was in 1995 for Mamaroneck, New York. This unit has a 104-foot aluminum ladder and a custom Sutphen tractor with a fully enclosed tilt-cab. The ladder rests high in the cradle with the handrails sitting just higher than the roof of the tiller cab. The fire department had Sutphen install two electric cord reels mounted along the side of the base section to supply power for auxiliary lights that could be deployed from the ladder.
Photo courtesy of Joel Gebet

The 1990s

In 1990, Pierce made changes to the tiller, eliminating the turntable leveling system, offering a fully enclosed cab for the tractor, and designing a new cab for the tillerman that was smaller than the original design. The tiller cab also had a bi-fold door replacing the single-hinged door. The front light bar on the tractor was mounted on a pair of brackets that raised it enough for the tillerman to see it for navigating.

One of the upgraded tillers was sold to Lowell, Massachusetts, and two were sold to Evanston, Illinois. After 1991, in response to NFPA 1904, a regulation regarding fire apparatus, the ladder rating was increased from 400 pounds to 500 pounds. One of the new units with a tandem-axle tractor was sold to Eugene, Oregon, and another went to Niles, Illinois, also with a tandem-axle tractor. Pierce sold a total of nine TDAs during their association with Smeal.

Seagrave built a small number of these heavy-duty, 100-foot tractor-drawn aerials in the mid-1980s. Cleveland took delivery of this unit with a fully enclosed custom cab and assigned it to Ladder 1 in 1984. They opted to have full-height cabinetry along the entire length of the trailer body for maximum storage. The heavier ladder is easily recognizable by the solid side panels on the base section that originate at the turntable, instead of the characteristic open sides that run the full length of the conventional Seagrave ladder. This aerial also required swing-out hydraulic stabilizers, whereas the other units had smaller, A-style jacks.

Sutphen introduced a new aerial in 1991—a 104-foot, mid-ship-mounted aerial ladder called the TS104. This was a 500-pound wet or dry, four-section aluminum ladder. Unlike their previous tower designs, this ladder had a three-sided design that eliminated the topside of the standard Sutphen box boom, providing an open walkway with high handrails. While other companies' ladders tapered the end of the fly section, each section of the TS104 was U-shaped and squared off over its full length. In 1992, Sutphen entered the tractor-drawn aerial market with a tillered version of the TS104. The tractor for the demo unit featured a custom Sutphen cab

mounted on an International chassis. Sutphen had a program at the time that combined their cabs with International chassis as a means of offering a lower cost chassis to customers. The first unit went to Nashville, Tennessee, in 1994. The second Sutphen tiller was built for Paterson, New Jersey, and used a tractor built by Spartan. Only one other TS104 tiller unit was delivered. In 1995, it was sold to Hook and Ladder Company Number 1 of Mamaroneck, New York, with a full Sutphen custom tractor unit.

Seagrave retired the Rear Admiral series and introduced the Patriot series aerials in 1992. These new ladders featured double-web, hollow I-beam

Baltimore City received several tractor-drawn 100-foot aerials in 1994 from Seagrave, one of which was assigned to Truck 7. The tractor features a large compartment behind the fully enclosed custom tilt-cab. Customary to Baltimore City rigs are the open transverse compartments on the bottom for the storage and easy access of long hand tools. Tucked up under the turntable are wheel chocks, which are used to secure the tractor's rear wheels when parking or deploying the rig.

construction base rails and provided Seagrave with a 250-pound-and-greater tip load. The Patriot series featured hydraulic extension cylinders for the ladder, replacing the winch-type extension on the Rear Admiral series. The 100-foot tractor-drawn ladder was part of the Patriot series. The first Patriot tiller went to Cicero, Illinois. The four-section, 100-foot TDAs had a pre-piped waterway option. Tillers built with a waterway required the installation of two mid-ship H-style outriggers, replacing the A-style outriggers on the standard aerial. With the introduction of the Patriot tiller, Seagrave no longer recommended that the tillers be jackknifed for deployment; rather, they recommended that the tractor and trailer be set in-line.

In 1995, LTI won the contract to provide Baltimore City's new tractor-drawn aerials. Truck 10 received one of these units, which had a Spartan custom tractor with a medium four-door (MFD) Gladiator cab. The 100-foot QS-100 ladder was painted gray, which was thought to be easier to keep clean. Previously, Baltimore tillers had two open lower compartments on the trailer for long hand tools. This new design retained those compartments but added roll-up doors and slide-out trays that could be accessed from either side of the rig, which kept firefighting tools cleaner by protecting them from the elements, but the city was even more interested in protecting the tools from theft by keeping them out of sight.

In 1993, Aerial Innovations (AI) entered the aerial market. AI's owners previously were with LTI before Simon purchased the company. They made aerials to be marketed in conjunction with a group of OEMs that did not have an aerial line to offer. Each product received a three-digit model designation. The first letter represented each specific aerial by the alphabetical order in which the company designed it. The second digit represented the number of ladder sections and the final letter denoted the mounting of the aerial as rear-mounted, midship, or tractor-drawn. The first product was the "A" ladder, a three-section, 75-foot heavy-duty aerial (A3R). This had a 500-pound rating, wet or dry.

In 1994, the B and the D series aerials were introduced. The D4M, D4R, and the D4T were

WHAT'S IN A NAME?

The term "hook and ladder" is generally associated with tractor-drawn aerial (TDA) fire apparatus by those outside the fire service, as well as by some within. In reality, the term is not exclusive to the TDA, but gained its origin in the late 1700s when the distinctions between types of fire units were the greatest.

During that time, the three types of fire units were the steam pumper, the hose wagon, and the hook and ladder. The steam pumper was responsible for pumping water through hoses to extinguish the fire; the hose wagon was tasked with getting the hose to the fire scene; and the hook and ladder arrived with other tools—hooks and ladders. "Ladder" refers to the ground ladders used to gain access to upper floors and to the roof. Because the term "hook and ladder" predates the permanent fixed master aerial device, it was not originally a defining characteristic. A pike pole—a metal hook attached to the end of a wooden pole—is a tool for pulling down walls and ceilings to provide access to the

fire and to check for fire in undetected areas. This tool, which was implemented many years ago, is still in everyday use. The first hook and ladders were not tillered rigs, though they required a steering tiller with the development of the main aerial ladder that was attached to the trailer.

Today, although almost every vehicle used for fire suppression carries ground ladders and pike poles, only aerial apparatus are considered hook and ladders. However, it is not uncommon for many fire departments to maintain tradition by using the hook and ladder designation or radio call sign for their straight-frame, non-tractor-drawn ladder trucks. Such is often the case during radio communications within the Chicago Fire Department. Units acknowledge the fire alarm office as a hook and ladder instead of as a truck. The St. Louis Fire Department runs an entire fleet of quints

In 1976 when this 100-foot rear-mounted Seagrave aerial was delivered to the Chicago Fire Department, they were still labeling truck companies as Hook & Ladders. This unit was Hook & Ladder Company 50 as indicated over the front wheel.

44

instead of the traditional engines and aerials. Each of the single-axle units is referred to as an engine—even though they have a permanent aerial device—and the longer tandem-axle aerials are called hook and ladders. These are not tractor-drawn but straight-frame units.

The early volunteer fire departments, called fire companies or clubs, gave themselves names to reflect their contribution to the fire service. Groups like the Washington Engine Company, Goodwill Fire Company, Willing Hand Hose Company, Dauntless Hook & Ladder Company, and Friendship Fire and Hose Company were formed in the early days of the fire service and maintain their incorporation and names to this day. Some may have changed their focus due to the needs of the community they serve, but continue to use the name on whatever vehicle they employ. One modern example is Cheltenham Hook & Ladder Company Number 1 of Cheltenham, Pennsylvania, which proudly exhibits the entire company name on their pumper.

In 1987, the St. Louis Fire Department embraced a new concept in firefighting and replaced their entire fleet of pumpers with quints. All of these units had 50-foot TeleSqurts or 75-foot LTI ladders on single-axle chassis and were labeled as engines. The department replaced their taller aerial devices in 1989 with 110-foot tandem-axle quints. These units had Spartan Monarch chassis with LTI QS-110 aerial ladders, 1,250-gallon-per-minute pumps, 200-gallon water tanks, 20-gallon foam tanks, preconnected attack lines, and a booster line. St. Louis labeled the tandem-axle aerial units "Hook & Ladders."

The FDNY refers to their aerial units as "tower ladders" when they have an Aerialscope boom, and as "ladders" when they have straight aerial ladders. For many years now, the entire fleet of rear-mounted and tractor-drawn aerial ladders in New York City have been built by Seagrave. Ladder 110, the Tillary Street Tigers, chose to keep tradition alive by adorning their 1994, 100-foot rear-mount with a beautiful sign plate proclaiming them as Hook & Ladder Company 110.

four-section, heavy-duty, 105-foot mid-mount, rear-mount, and tractor-drawn aerials with 500-pound ratings, wet or dry. They used four H-style jacks with a 16-foot spread. The first 105-foot aerial was a D4T with bodywork by RD Murray for the District Heights Fire Department in Landover, Maryland.

Also in 1994, LTI introduced the AH-100 and the AH-110 rear-mount aerials that were a new design. Both were offered with pre-piped waterways. The AH-100 had a 750-pound dry rating and a 600-pound wet rating. Both ladders had four sections, although the 110-foot ladder had longer sections. The 100-foot model allowed for a shorter overall vehicle. When built without a pump, the ladder would not extend past the bumper in the travel position. When built with a pump and extended cab, the ladder would not extend past the windshield. Jack spread was 16 feet, with four H-style outriggers. Shortly after the rear-mounts were introduced, LTI offered an AH-100 tractor-drawn ladder. A 750-pound AH-series ladder was easily distinguished at a glance from other ladders due to the triangulated lifting configuration (TLC), which incorporated a triangular-shaped steel frame along the side of the

In 1994, Huntington Beach, California, specified a tiller quint to increase the effectiveness of their resources. Simon-LTI won the contract and built this 90-foot, QS-90 aerial with a D8400 medium four-door (MFD) custom tractor built by their sister company, Simon-Duplex. The tractor was fitted with a 1,500-gallon-per-minute mid-ship pump and a 187-gallon water tank. The trailer has full-height, rescue-style compartments with roll-up doors. The attack lines were built into the trailer near the outriggers.

After they begin to build ladders themselves, Pierce constructed two of their first tractor-drawn aerials in 1996. Both feature different configurations of Lance tractors. One, for Hyattsville, Maryland, has an extra-long cab with a raised roof; the other, for Long Beach, California, has a standard four-door cab with a flat roof and short, barrier-clearing doors. Differing from the Smeal design previously sold by Pierce, the new ladders slope down toward the tiller cab and rest well below the driver's line of sight. Both aerials are pre-piped and have similar body designs. The Hyattsville unit has a handrail for added safety outside the tiller cab. Both cabs have different door configurations for the tiller cab, a single-hinged door for Long Beach and a hinged bi-fold door for Hyattsville.

LAFD Truck 96 is stationed in the hills near the Ventura County line. The rig is a 1995 100-foot model QS-100 aerial by Simon-LTI with a Simon-Duplex model D8400 cab and tractor. The narrow tiller cab features drop-down windows that allow the tillerman to stick his head out of the window for increased visibility. Some fire departments specify a plexiglass bubble window for this purpose, but plexiglass has a tendency to scratch, which eventually limits visibility.

base section surrounding the lift cylinder. These units required two sets of H-style outriggers with a 16-foot spread. In addition, LTI initiated a system of inserting four rods around the fifth wheel to lock the tractor and trailer together into a rigid unit.

LTI built their first full tiller quint in 1994, for Huntington Beach, California. This was a QS-90 aerial with a 1,500-gallon-per-minute mid-ship pump and a 187-gallon water tank added to the tractor. As the quint concept gained in popularity, fire departments began to look for solutions to a desire for a pump and tank in addition to the maneuverability of the TDA. Another tiller quint was built shortly thereafter for Encinitas, California, followed by a PTO quint for Vancouver,

Washington, in 1995 and another full tiller quint for Kirkland, Washington, in 1997.

Pierce replaced the 105-foot TDA, which had been out of the line since they left Smeal in 1991, with a new medium-duty 100-foot model in 1994. This was a four-section aerial with a 250-pound tip load at 0 degrees and a 500-pound rating above 39 degrees. Pierce no longer used the swing-out stabilizers, opting instead for one set of H-style outriggers with a 16-foot spread located behind the turntable. The first new Pierce tiller was sold in 1995 to Gainesville, Georgia.

In 1996, KME received a large order for fire apparatus from the Los Angeles County Fire Department. To fill it, KME had to modify a three-section,

In 1996, Indianapolis took delivery of this QH-100 tractor-drawn aerial from Simon-LTI. This heavy-duty LTI ladder has a 500-pound tip load, and was assigned as Truck 31. There are two easy ways to identify this as the QH ladder at a glance. First, there are four outriggers: one set is located in the customary spot on the trailer and the second set is on the tractor. Second, the attachment point for the lift cylinders is at the top rail of the base section. Lift cylinders for the 250-pound QS ladder attach at the bottom edge of the base section. This aerial has a pre-piped waterway and an electric cord reel near the tip to supply power into or onto the roof of a fire building. The tractor is a custom Simon-Duplex with a D9400 cab.

75-foot aerial, and mount it on a trailer to build their first TDA. They also mounted a pump-and-water tank onto the tractor to produce a tiller quint. This shared the 500-pound wet and dry ratings of a single-axle, 75-foot, rear-mount with the same two outriggers and 14-foot jack spread. Nine of these units were built for Los Angeles County and delivered in 1998. KME followed the 75-foot TDA with a four-section, 100-foot model. They added a heavier base section under the three-section, 75-foot aerial, which gave them a 500-pound dry rating and a 250-pound wet rating. The first 100-foot TDA went to South County, California, in 1998 and then four

were delivered to Los Angeles County in 1999. The 100-foot uses two H-style outriggers with a 16-foot jack spread. Both the 75-foot and the 100-foot units can carry up to 300 gallons of water and are offered with pumps having capacities of up to 2,250 gallons per minute.

In 1998, E-ONE entered the TDA market. This new product used an HP100 ladder mounted on a tiller chassis. E-ONE had to engineer and adapt the Cyclone II chassis to accommodate a fifth-wheel assembly to pull the trailer. The tiller utilizes one pair of H-style jacks mounted at the base of the turntable behind the tractor with a spread of 17 feet, 6 inches.

In 1998 at the Fire Rescue International trade show in Louisville, Sutphen introduced a tractor-drawn platform aerial called the 2000+ platform tiller. This is the four-section, 100-foot, box-boom aluminum ladder from their popular mid-mount tower. It has a different bucket, though, with a unique platform design that acts as the housing for the tillerman when the ladder is bedded. The bucket floor becomes the ceiling for the tillerman's cab. Once on-scene, the roof of the cab raises up for deployment of the tower and becomes the platform, which has a pre-piped gun on either side of the bucket like the mid-mount towers. The trailer has one pair of H-style outriggers; the body was built with many compartments using roll-up doors, and is pulled by a custom Sutphen tractor.

The ladder has a 500-pound tip-load rating, wet or dry. Although the comparable HP100 rear-mounted aerial uses two pair of E-ONE crisscross scissors-style jacks with a spread of only 12 feet, designers thought the tiller would be better designed with only one set of outriggers to simplify spotting the rig on tight streets. In order to provide the same stability, this set has a wider stance of 17 feet, 6 inches. Five tillers were purchased by the fire department in Kansas City, Missouri, as part of an order that totaled more than 30 units including pumpers and rescues. The next customer was the San Bruno Fire Department in California, which bought a tiller and a matching pumper in 2001, followed by the Baltimore County Fire Department, which purchased a tiller in 2002.

Sutphen introduced a TDA platform called the 2000+ platform tiller at the Fire Rescue International trade show in Louisville in 1998. This four-section, 100-foot aluminum ladder had a unique platform design that acted as the housing for the tillerman when the ladder was bedded. The bucket floor became the ceiling for the tillerman's cab, with the roof rising at the scene for deployment and transformation into the bucket.

The tractor-drawn aerials that LTI offered in the late 1990s included the QS-series 250-pound medium-duty, QH-series 500-pound heavy-duty, plus the AH-series TLC 750-pound extra-heavy-duty ladders. Stabilizers varied with spreads of as little as 14 feet by using two H-style outriggers with

This 1997 LTI tractor-drawn aerial from Newport Beach, California, is a model QS-90 with a 250-pound tip load. The tractor is a Spartan Gladiator with an MFD cab. The 90-foot ladder has a pre-piped waterway and the trailer is fitted with roll-up doors for the rescue-style compartments. The upper compartments at the rear of the trailer are covered with diamond plate for durability, instead of a painted surface, which is susceptible to scratching. The yellow cord reel behind the cab is connected to a generator for powering electric lights and tools.

four lockout cylinders to secure the fifth wheel of the tractor. These cylinders tied the tractor and trailer together, providing a more stable base than the standard two outriggers with a 16-foot spread. AH ladders used four outriggers with a 16-foot spread or the optional swing-out style outriggers, which were less popular.

In 1998 Freightliner purchased LTI, several years after purchasing the name and assets of American LaFrance. After integrating the LTI products under the American LaFrance brand, LTI announced new product designations. Among the TDAs, the QH became the L23T-100, the AH series ladders became the L34T-100 and the L34T-110, while the QS series became the L14T-90 and the L14T-100.

The 2000s

In 2000, Seagrave built a PTO tiller quint for Empire Hook and Ladder Company Number 1, in Upper Nyack, New York. This 100-foot Patriot

One of the first LTI tractor-drawn aerials with an American LaFrance tractor and raised MFD Eagle cab was assigned to Ladder 15 in Philadelphia and delivered in 1998. The city bought many of these units. The ladder is a QS-100 and the trailer was ordered with roll-up doors.

tiller had a 200-gallon water tank, preconnected attack lines, and a 250-gallon-per-minute PTO pump added to the rear of the tractor. Since the unit had a PTO pump, rather than a full mid-ship pump, the TDA was not credited as being a full quint.

As of this writing, R.K. Aerials designers are in the process of making product enhancements to increase the tip load of the straight aerial ladders from 500 pounds to 750 pounds. They are also designing a four-section, 100-foot, tractor-drawn aerial with a 500-pound tip load and possibly a tiller quint to follow.

The Patriot series, by Seagrave, consists of the three-section, 75-foot rear-mount Mean Stick, the four-section 100-foot rear-mount, and 100-foot TDA. The Patriot TDA has a 250-pound tip load. It is offered with a pre-piped, pinnable waterway, which requires the optional H-style outriggers with a 17-foot spread. Otherwise, the TDA uses two compact A-style jacks. Either way, stabilizers on the TDA are located at the front section of the trailer body. Seagrave is working on implementing a 500-pound tractor-drawn aerial in response to market demands. When completed, a tiller with a 500-pound tip load will require two sets of H-style outriggers and the ability to lock the fifth wheel for added rigidity.

As of July 2001, Aerial Innovations stopped accepting orders for aerial devices, and in November 2001 the AI line was discontinued. As part of the American LaFrance family, AI found it increasingly difficult to offer a product to OEMs that could compete with American LaFrance units featuring the LTI aerials. During the period between 1993 and 2001, AI built 24 tractor-drawn aerials, which were sold through 3D, Becker, General Safety, Luverne, Quality, RD Murray, and Westates. The 500-pound D4T accounted for 19 units and the other five units had the 250-pound C4T ladder, including one tiller quint for the University of California Fire Department at the Davis campus.

In 2002, the first tiller quint carrying the American LaFrance name was delivered to Lodi, California. Although the unit was built by LTI, the LTI product name has been absorbed into the American LaFrance line.

Empire Hook & Ladder Company Number 1 of Upper Nyack, New York, currently runs the only Seagrave PTO tiller quint. This truck is the third PTO tiller quint that has served this department. Delivered in 2000, the new truck has the first Seagrave tractor to feature a fully enclosed custom tilt-cab with a raised roof. The tractor incorporates preconnected attack lines, a 250-gallon-per-minute PTO pump, and a 200-gallon water tank. Uncommon to fire departments on the East Coast, this aerial has wooden ground ladders. *Photo courtesy of Joel Gebet*

The York City Fire Department in Pennsylvania received this tractor-drawn, 105-foot model D4T aerial in 1999. The four-section ladder was built by Aerial Innovations; the bodywork was fabricated by 3D Fire Apparatus of Shawano, Wisconsin; and the custom tractor is by American LaFrance with a raised MFD Eagle cab. The tiller cab has angled corners with small windows to increase the tillerman's visibility. Unlike many tillers, this trailer was designed with four rescue-style, full-height compartments. Another feature is Aerial Innovations' use of two sets of hydraulic H-style outriggers—one on the tractor and the other at the front of the trailer. Complications with this unit arose and the fire department ultimately chose not to put the unit into service and replaced it with a rear-mounted ladder.

Truck 21 is a 1997 Pierce 100-foot TDA from Glendale, California. The tractor features a Quantum cab with air-operated steps that fold down when the doors are opened and then automatically retract when the doors are closed. The tractor was ordered with storage compartments behind the cab for added capacity. This was the fourth tractor-drawn aerial Pierce built after introducing their new aerial ladder.

Chapter Three

DESIGN AND COMPONENTS

What's the Romance?

There are many reasons for purchasing a tiller—and there are reasons not to do so. On the plus side, a tiller is the most maneuverable aerial device available—period (depending on whom you talk to). The articulating joint combined with the rear-steering axle and an experienced driver and tillerman allow the unit to go almost anywhere, forward or backward. Consider first that the front steering axle on the tractor can have a 45-degree wheel cut—similar to what can be offered on a conventional rear-mount. Add to that a fifth-wheel hinge point capable of a virtual 90-degree pivot, meaning that the truck can actually pivot within its own length. Complete the package with a steerable rear axle that can alter the path of the rear to conform to curves or can straighten out to follow the front. The result is superior maneuverability when compared to straight-frame trucks. An average 100-foot rear-mounted aerial with a 232-inch wheelbase has a turning radius of 37 1/2 feet. A comparable 100-foot tiller with a tractor wheelbase of 141 inches has a turning radius of 22 feet, 10 inches, and is a considerably longer vehicle. The long design of the tiller also provides for a lower center of gravity when compared to a rear-mount where the ladder is mounted higher and rests over the cab of the truck.

Hotels, office complexes, and condominium and townhouse developments with tight turns, crowded parking lots, and narrow streets are modern locations that are well served by maneuverable, tractor-drawn aerials. Several years ago, their benefits had been largely ignored, with a few exceptions, by all but the oldest cities and towns with their narrow streets. As urban areas grew, streets became wider, and suburbs expanded into wide-open spaces with roads that had plenty of room. The need for a tiller's mobility diminished in many places. Cities like New York greatly reduced the number of tillers they used. Washington, D.C., purchased rear-mounted ladders for the first time in 60 years. Baltimore experimented with mid-mounted tower ladder quints. These are but three examples suggesting a decline of tractor-drawn aerials. Some areas, of course, will continue to require a TDA for access, although they have become far fewer than in the past.

Another benefit of the TDA over a straight-frame truck is the ability to store vast amounts of equipment. The trailer provides tremendous compartment space when compared to a tandem-axle rear-mounted aerial. Large transverse compartments accessible from either side of the vehicle are considerably larger than what conventional trucks offer with shallower compartments that are constrained by the torque box, water tank, and rear axles. The tiller body is longer than the body of a rear-mount

so that even if both had compartments of the same size, the tiller's added length would still guarantee more space. In some fire departments, there is never enough room to carry all of the required equipment. A rear-mount can offer perhaps 200 cubic feet of space, whereas a tiller can provide up to 400 cubic feet—twice as much. Having a tiller generally means that the fire department can carry everything it wants. The tractor-drawn aerial also provides

This is a rear view of a modern Pierce tiller. The cab is narrow and allows the driver to easily lower either window to peer out. The rear window slides open for ventilation. Ground ladder storage is behind the roll-up door. The tillerman gains access to the cab via stairs cut into the body with the help of several grab rails positioned along the way.

additional ground ladder storage. This is especially important to fire departments that make an aggressive use of ladders on the fire ground. Many rear-mounts carry 115 feet of ground ladders, which is the minimum required by the National Fire Protection Association (NFPA), up to a maximum of 163 feet. Tillers can accommodate in excess of 270 feet of ladders, including the largest ladders, which would take up too much room in a rear-mount.

Perhaps the final item in the plus category for owning a tiller is that they're just plain fun to drive—whether en route to a fire or in a parade.

On the minus side, a major item is cost. In order to properly staff a TDA, the company should include a driver, officer, two firefighters, and the tillerman. For many departments, a five-man truck company, or even a four-man company, is not an option. Staffing for all but a few departments is at a maximum of four, and often less. Hiring additional firefighters per shift presents a significant long-term expense for management. When manpower concerns affect the existence of a tiller, generally it is the large union departments that succeed in keeping the personnel, whereas many smaller departments are unable to mount a successful challenge.

The cost of a TDA is higher than a straight-frame aerial ladder even if the straight-frame unit is equipped as a quint with a pump-and-water tank. Using rough numbers, a 100-foot rear-mounted aerial with a 500-pound tip load and no pump can cost between $500,000 and $575,000. A comparable tractor-drawn aerial can cost from $600,000 to $670,000. The numbers on either side increase by $30,000 to $40,000 for a quint with a water tank and mid-ship pump. Construction of a tiller is considerably more labor-intensive than a rear-mount. The longer body is more involved, and the fifth-wheel assembly along with the rear-steering axle and the tillerman's cab all add time, materials, and expense.

The proliferation of straight-frame aerials with computerized rear-steering capabilities that are controlled by the driver provide another reason for the replacement of TDAs by some fire departments. Such straight-frame aerials can maintain the required maneuverability, reduce the manpower required, and put a full quint in service.

The Tiller Cab

The tillerman's cab has changed quite a bit. The first tillers simply had a seat with a steering wheel. Some of the earliest models placed the seat below the main ladder, while others were on top. The

This is another view of a Pierce tiller cab, with added rear and side handrails for safety. On the rear of the cab, below the window, is an arrow stick directional light bar. Once on-scene, the series of yellow lights is set to create an arrow showing traffic the proper way to go around the truck. There is a bus fan mounted in front of the driver and both of the lower compartments feature slide-out shelving to facilitate access to the equipment that will be carried. This unit has wooden ground ladders and a conventional aerial ladder without a pre-piped waterway.

The Portland, Oregon, Bureau of Fire, Rescue, and Emergency Services operates seven tractor-drawn aerials. This unit was delivered in 1998 with a 100-foot, LTI QS-100 ladder that has a 250-pound tip load. The tractor by American LaFrance has a medium four-door Eagle cab and is outfitted with proprietary rooftop light bars that were designed specifically for American LaFrance by Whelen. Sticking straight up toward the rear of the tractor cab is a pole-mounted boat light that allows the tillerman to gauge the location of the truck cab. An aluminum ladder provides access to the tiller cab, which features a plexiglass bubble window in the cab door to protect the tillerman from Portland's rainy climate.

seat had to swing out of the way in order to deploy the ladder, until American LaFrance introduced the four-section ladder in the late 1930s. The additional ladder section meant that each could be shorter, which allowed the tillerman's seat to be placed in a permanent position out of the ladder's way. It took several years before the industry abandoned the three-section designs without the fixed tillerman's seat. Manufacturers began offering a windshield for the tillerman in the mid-1930s and early 1940s. The tillerman remained out in the open until the late 1970s and early 1980s, when apparatus builders began to build a completely enclosed tillerman's cab with a roof and doors.

The tiller cab today offers several options to upgrade the driver's working environment. Although all companies provide power steering and heat, some include air conditioning, bus fans, a sunroof for added visibility, and headsets for verbal communication with the driver, instead of the older buzzer system with predetermined codes. A tilting and telescopic steering wheel is optional along with exterior spotlights and ground illumination for added safety at night. Another item to help the tillerman is a wheel alignment indicator to make sure that the operator knows which direction the wheels are facing, since the steering wheel is capable of turning three and a half times around. Competing manufacturers offer different widths for the cab along with various seats to enhance the tillerman's comfort. A training seat is also requested on many tillers. This is a small seat mounted inside the cab or outside, depending on cab width. It enables an experienced tiller operator to safely accompany a driver with less training while acting as an instructor. This seat is not intended for use while responding to an emergency, and when placed outside the cab it is often removable.

An option that used to be widely requested was a clear plexiglass bubble window on the sides of the tiller cab. These would allow the tillerman to stick his head out slightly to gain better forward visibility while still being protected from the elements. This feature is not as widely used today, largely because the plexiglass was susceptible to scratching that would eventually make visibility extremely difficult. As a substitute, American

Top: E-ONE designed their tiller cab wider in the rear and tapered toward the front to give the driver better forward visibility through the angled door. Since the doors face forward, they are equipped with windshield wipers like the front windshield. The door also has a truck-style vent panel, which when opened, allows air to flow into the cab for comfort. E-ONE also designed a different type of step layout for the tillerman to gain access to the cab or the ladder.

Left: The wider tiller cab design by E-ONE allows ample space to include the buddy seat inside the cab; most competitors mount the seat outside.

LaFrance offers a drop-down window in each tiller cab door. This allows the tillerman to stick his head out of the window if necessary on occasions when he might be tempted to drive with the door open for a better vantage. In order for this to be practical, the width of the tiller cab is narrower than some, or it would be too far to reach the window on one side and difficult for the tillerman to stick his head out the window while steering. Fire departments in areas where the climate produces a significant amount of snow or rain still specify the bubble to provide protection for the tillerman.

The tillerman's visibility is constrained in several directions. To the front, the tillerman is looking through the bedded aerial ladder from a slightly elevated position. It can be difficult to judge the front of the cab at night or in inclement weather. The builders incorporate some system of lights on the cab roof for this reason. One option is a boat light mounted to the tractor roof to allow the tillerman to gain a perspective relative to the cab. Sometimes turn signals and brake light indicators are part of this display. The tillerman is also constrained in seeing down to the street or curb along either side of the trailer. The design of the body and the mounting of equipment can complicate this. High side compartments on the trailer can also be an obstruction: the further these are mounted rearward, the more they hinder the tillerman's visibility. A general rule of thumb is that the compartments should stop halfway back or no more than a maximum of two thirds of the way to the rear of the trailer. Most often, fans, ladders, or other loose equipment are mounted in the remaining space. Although ladders are a slight hindrance to visibility, the tillerman can usually see through or around them to view the street and curb. Newer tiller cabs offered by American LaFrance and KME have substituted seamed glass for the cab front and rear, eliminating the

corner posts to provide the maximum amount of unobstructed glass for the driver. Philadelphia utilizes a camera mounted on each side of the trailer body to enhance the tillerman's visibility, along with two small video monitors in the tiller cab for viewing. Each camera is located in a place that eliminates the blind spot near the tillerman's rear wheel, which

Here is a modern Seagrave tiller cab on a 1993 TDA from San Bernardino, California. Access to the cab is on the other side of the trailer. This is another narrow cab design with a bus fan and lower door vents to help cool the driver in the summer heat. The cab door slides to the rear to open. San Bernardino uses aluminum ground ladders, though some California departments prefer wood.

allows a complete view along the side of the body showing parked cars and other obstacles.

Access to the tiller cab is gained by climbing steps at the rear of the trailer. Depending on the equipment to be mounted and the preference of the fire department, the tail end of either side can accommodate a ladder with a full handrail similar to a rear-mount, or, in the case of departments like the city of Los Angeles that mounts ladders all the way back, individual steps can be mounted to the body, spaced so that they are in the voids around the mounted equipment. A set of handrails along the top of the body provides a grab hold. The doors to the cab can be hinged or sliding.

The Outriggers

As with any aerial device, a tillered ladder has to be stabilized before deployment. The turntable—the rotating base anchoring the ladder—is located at the front of the trailer, above the fifth-wheel hookup—the pivot point for the vehicle while driving. Stability for ladder operations comes from two sources: the stiffness of the chassis frame of both the tractor and trailer, and the stabilizing jacks, which provide lateral support to prevent the vehicle from tipping over. The jacks are most often bolted to the frame rails at a 90-degree angle. Although most tillers require only one set of jacks—one jack on each side of the unit—some are built with two sets.

The earliest tillers from American LaFrance, Pirsch, and Seagrave required the tractor to be jackknifed to the trailer for additional lateral support. The stabilizers on these units were located at the front portion of the trailer and consisted of one or two pair of manually operated jacks. Most often these were gravity-fed screw-type jacks that would corkscrew or simply drop downward to the ground of their own weight after being pulled away or swung out from the body and released.

continued on page 66

Atlanta operates 9 tractor-drawn aerials out of 14 total aerials in service. In 1991, they purchased several tillers from LTI with the QH-110, 500-pound, 110-foot ladders. When this aerial was introduced in 1988, it required an 18-foot jack spread, which was wider than the trailer body could accommodate with conventional straight out-and-down stabilizers. To overcome this obstacle, LTI utilized swing-out-and-down jacks. A hydraulic arm pushes the leg out in an arc until it is perpendicular to the trailer body. After the vertical beam in the leg is lowered to the ground, a steel pin is inserted in the arm as a locking mechanism and another is placed through the vertical beam for safety. Both pins, which are visible, are stored along the jacks near the points where they are deployed. Metal wheel chocks are used in front of and behind the rear tires of the tractor to prevent the truck from rolling.

REAR STEERING

The maneuverability of tractor-drawn aerial apparatus has been known throughout the fire service for almost 200 years. There have been several attempts to match this maneuverability or in some cases to simply improve on the maneuverability of straight-frame apparatus with rear-steering systems. FWD offered a steerable rear axle for Seagrave aerials in the late 1960s and extended this to other manufacturers in the years following. This all-wheel steering was limited to low speeds and was particularly designed to aid in apparatus placement on the fire ground. The FWD system used single rear axles with single wheels.

Provo, Utah, purchased five new Pierce rigs in 2001 including two, 105-foot rear-mounted aerials on Quantum chassis with Pierce's ALL STEER electronic steering system for maneuverability. Truck 5, pictured here in front of the breathtaking backdrop of the Rocky Mountains, is positioned showing the coordinated fire-ground mode where the rear wheels are turned opposite of the front wheels to permit the tightest of turning options. The rearmost axle has a greater angle than the forward tandem as calculated by the computerized system based on the degree of turn by the driver. The decal above the driver's handrail represents Provo's participation in the 2002 Winter Olympic Games. Provo hosted the venue for ice hockey.

Tag Axles

In 1993, Spartan Motors, a custom chassis company, offered a steerable rear tag axle for tighter turning. This was introduced in conjunction with S&S, a body builder that wanted to market this product for elliptical tankers. S&S called it the Twin Steer. Unlike the FWD system, this product used tandem rear axles, the front of which had dual wheels while the rearmost, the tag axle, used large single wheels. This design required no action on the part of the driver. The rearmost axle turned in the opposite direction of the front axle to follow the turn. This was a non-driving axle, and the rear steering functioned while moving forward or in reverse. At speeds in excess of 25 miles per hour, the axle locked straight.

Spartan then offered this system to all of their customers, simply calling it a trailing tag axle, with no other marketing name. This was incorporated into rescue squads and tankers, but the primary usage was for aerial devices. The maximum rear axle weight in combination that it was capable of carrying was 44,000 pounds, enough for straight aerial ladders with lengths of up to 100 feet. Rear-mounted 100-foot ladder towers were too heavy to use the trailing tag axle. Aerial Innovations, LTI, RK, and Smeal were some of the companies that built aerials with this system, placing units into such locations as Toronto, Ontario; Cutlerville, Michigan; and San Jose, California. In 2000, Spartan's supplier for the trailing tag axle discontinued the product and, as a result, so did Spartan.

In 1995, Simon-Duplex, another custom chassis company, which is no longer in business, offered a steerable rear tag axle made by Ridewell. This system also did not require any intervention on the part of the driver. It could automatically sense a turn and follow along to decrease the turning radius. The rear axles would lock straight again when the front wheels came out of the turn. This system functioned with the vehicle moving forward or in reverse. Like Spartan's system, the Simon-Duplex package was most often used for aerials.

American LaFrance, HME, and KME Fire Apparatus currently have steerable tag axle packages available. Again, as required by any other tag axle configuration, these designs utilize a dual-wheel rear-drive axle in front of a single-wheel tag axle. In each case, the tag axle is free-floating, following a turn and decreasing the turning radius. Demand for these tag axles has been minimal for these companies, with KME having only installed it on a few 75-foot rear-mounted aerials and American LaFrance building a handful of aerials with it. These are not as maneuverable as an electronic rear-steering system. Ridewell, Granning, and Watson & Chanlin are companies that supply the steerable tag axles to the general trucking industry, a small part of which represents the fire service, although Ridewell has recently stopped offering their product to the fire service.

The tag axle is not a substitute for a unit that requires full tandem axles for the vehicle weight; however, it is an option for improving the turning radius while at the same time offering some added weight distribution where the full tandem is not required. The tag axle itself is rated for weights of between 10,000 and 12,000 pounds, significantly less than a dual-wheel axle. The tag axle costs between $5,000 and $7,000, whereas a second drive axle with dual wheels would cost between $10,000 and $12,000.

ALL STEER

In 1994, the Oshkosh Truck Corporation introduced their ALL STEER® computerized all-wheel steering system for Pierce fire apparatus. Although it was new to the fire service, the all-wheel steering had been available on specialty Oshkosh vehicles for well over 50 years. This is

The City of San Bernardino, California, has many units built by Pierce including Truck 221—a 1998, 105-foot rear-mounted straight-truck company. This unit is built on a Dash 2000 chassis and is equipped with the ALL STEER electronic steering system. San Bernardino City also runs a tractor-drawn aerial. Truck 221 is shown making what at first glance might seem an unremarkable right-hand turn. What the ALL STEER system is demonstrating here is a right turn into an alley from the curb lane that does not require the driver to first swing left into the next lane. The driver though has to be careful of where the rear end swings during this turn so as not to clip a car in the next lane.

available for either single-axle or tandem-axle apparatus—using single wheels for both. Unlike tag axles that simply follow, ALL STEER provides additional maneuverability because it actually steers. Each of the steering axles is a driving axle,

which means that the tandem-axle ALL STEER unit has all of the benefits of both tandem axles in terms of weight distribution and traction. Unlike the tag axle, which must be positioned behind a drive axle, the single rear-axle ALL STEER can lend excellent maneuverability to a lighter piece of apparatus. Pumpers, tankers, rescues, aerial platforms, and aerial ladders have been fitted with ALL STEER.

Offering up to a 30 percent reduction in turning radius over conventional trucks, the ALL STEER has three steering modes: standard (or front steering), coordinated, and fire ground. Each mode allows the driver to determine what is needed to best negotiate tight turns during response or maneuvers for placement of the apparatus when on-scene. The driver decides when to engage the system and chooses the steering mode. Then, the computerized system automatically calculates the correct wheel angles as the driver turns the steering wheel.

The standard setting is no different from a conventional vehicle where the front wheels turn and the rear wheels are locked in a straight line with the chassis.

Coordinated steering enables the rear wheels to turn opposite of the front wheels for the tightest available turning radius, and works at speeds of between 2 and 35 miles per hour. At higher speeds, the steering remains in the standard mode for safety.

Fire-ground mode offers two options: First, there is a coordinated option, which at lower fire-ground speeds provides sharper angles from the rear wheels than at higher speeds. Second is the crab mode, which turns the rear wheels the same direction as the front wheels, allowing the rig to shift forward or backward along a 45-degree diagonal line. With this setting the driver can get close to the curb quickly without making several maneuvers, or get in front of another vehicle without having to move the other rig. In 1996, Oshkosh purchased Pierce, fully integrating the ALL STEER into the Pierce product line with the Saber, Dash, Lance, Enforcer, and Quantum series chassis.

Independent Comparison

In 1999, a fire department in Oregon set up their own controlled tests comparing a tandem-axle straight aerial truck equipped with Pierce's ALL STEER to a tractor-drawn aerial with a driver and tillerman. After purchasing one unit equipped with ALL STEER and prior to making a decision on purchasing their next aerial device, the apparatus committee wanted to compare maneuverability between the two types of aerials. Tractor-drawn aerials were common to the area and they wanted to make an informed choice. In doing so, they tried to include a variety of obstacles that were common to their district, such as a tight parking lot, turns on narrow streets with parked cars, and a tight back-up maneuver. During the tests, the TDA was unable to clear all of the obstacles without stopping and backing up, while the ALL STEER navigated the entire test route without stopping. After the demonstration was over, the fire department that sponsored this trial went on to stipulate that a more experienced driver and tillerman might have been able to navigate the course without stopping. Pierce was undoubtedly pleased with the independent results.

Although the Oregon test applied to aerial apparatus only, the ALL STEER is commonplace on smaller rigs for gaining similar access to tight spots. Increasingly, navigating driveways and shopping centers as well as residential streets with parked cars can present maneuverability problems for some of today's larger pumpers, rescues, and tankers. Departments can reduce navigation difficulties by specifying smaller rigs with shorter cabs that offer tight cramp angles, and by shortening the bodies. However, these solutions can compromise the available storage space for the vast equipment that some fire departments require, as well as reduce the size of the water tank. Another option is to increase vehicle maneuverability with ALL STEER or a steerable tag axle.

Later versions were hydraulically operated A-style jacks, radial arm jacks, or H-style jacks. The A-style supports were angled at 45 degrees toward the ground, and when deployed, they extended to the ground and did not protrude very far past the width of the trailer. The radial arm jacks were stored in a vertical position along the trailer, with the footpads up in the air. When activated, a cylinder would push the arm over toward the ground, where the pad would then come to rest on the pavement. The H-style jacks have a horizontal beam that retracts into the body for storage and extends away from the body for deployment. Attached to the end of these beams are vertical legs consisting of one beam within a larger one that is lowered to the ground. H-style jacks extend further from the trailer body than A-style jacks, thereby widening the overall stance of the vehicle during aerial operations and offering greater stability against overturning.

Most builders' jack options now include the H-style, also known as out-and-down outriggers. This wider base increases the working range and weight-carrying capacity of the ladder, allowing for cantilevered support at all angles of elevation. Some builders use a second set of H-style outriggers to further increase the ladder's tip-load rating. Use of a second pair also reduces the distance or spread of the first set and minimizes the total amount of space required on the fire ground to set up the aerial.

One method of designing the H-style outriggers was to have them swing out in an arc to a pre-set distance instead of telescoping from the side. Pierce, Seagrave, and LTI employed this type of

The out-and-down hydraulic outriggers on this Pierce tiller are positioned at the front of the trailer along with the stabilizer controls. The narrow gauge below the sign plate is used to determine level when deploying the jacks. This truck is also equipped with a pre-piped waterway and electric cord reels. The waterway is fed via the inlets located on either side of the rig, under the stabilizer controls.

jack on some of their tillers. The biggest drawback to this design is that it requires a larger area to deploy because the full arc of swing to 90 degrees must be clear; telescoping jacks, by contrast, can be positioned to extend between obstacles. The early Seagrave swing-out jacks were manually operated and later jacks were hydraulically driven. The LTI and Pierce swing-out jacks were always hydraulic.

This is an example of the first generation of tractor-drawn aerial offered by Pierce in 1988, and sold to Pittsburgh, Pennsylvania. Smeal built the 105-foot steel ladder under an exclusive licensing arrangement with Pierce. The modified Dash cab had an elevated rear roof with running lights for the benefit of the tillerman and added headroom for the firefighters who used the jump seats. This design had a leveling system for the turntable capable of adjusting to a 10-degree front-to-back angle and 4 degrees from side to side. The turntable was hinged to the trailer, which allowed the pedestal to be leveled with the horizon regardless of the trailer position. The mechanism to implement this leveling raised the turntable, which in turn raised the entire ladder when it was stored. This higher position placed the handrails of the bedded ladder above the cab of the tractor, causing the need for the raised roof panel on the tractor. The outriggers were a swing-out design implemented with hydraulic cylinders.

LTI used the swing-out stabilizers when they introduced their QH series of 500-pound tip-load ladders in 1994. These were necessary because the engineers determined that an 18-foot jack spread was needed to achieve the desired stability and to meet NFPA requirements. LTI wanted to maintain a single pair of outriggers rather than two sets. An 18-foot total spread is measured as 9 feet to either side of the center of the truck frame. This would mean that 9

feet of jack had to retract into the body for storage. The swing-out design allowed LTI to move the jack forward of the gooseneck, whereas any retractable jack had to be rearward of the turntable in order to find a place on the trailer body to house it. The forward position of the swing-out jack put the point of stabilization at the very front of the gooseneck, in front of the fifth wheel, yielding greater stability for ladder operations over the front of the truck. To deploy the swing-out LTI outrigger, a hydraulic cylinder pushes the arm out to a preset position. A pin is then inserted to lock the arm in place and a steel sleeve is placed over the cylinder.

Both Aerial Innovations and LTI, followed by American LaFrance—after the acquisition of LTI—designed tillers with two sets of H-style outriggers. The second set allows LTI to increase the tip-load rating of their 500-pound ladder to 750 pounds, and Aerial Innovations to bump their 250-pound ladder to 500 pounds. Both of these aerials with the heavier configurations also used a set of four cylinders around the fifth wheel to lock the tractor and trailer together to prevent flexing or articulation at the fifth-wheel connection. Modern tillers no longer require the tractor to be jackknifed for added stability; in fact, most now specify that the tractor and trailer be in line.

This is the view looking forward from the tiller cab of an E-ONE tractor-drawn aerial. The two yellow lights give the driver a perspective of the location of the tractor in order to judge distance and assist with navigation. Visible on the left side, inside the aluminum ladder, are mountings that contain an axe and a pike pole. By storing these items near the tip of the aerial, the roof man can climb the ladder more quickly, without having to hold onto the tools. Once near the top, the tools are easily accessible for rapid deployment.

E-ONE uses an integral torque box and chassis frame, which permits a lower center of gravity for their aerials. Less relevant to a tiller than a rear-mounted device, the lower center of gravity combined with E-ONE's lighter aluminum ladder allows for a narrower jack spread on the fire ground. The integral torque box and chassis frame also allows for a higher resistance to bending moment (a technical term meaning that the frame resists twisting to a greater degree). When an aerial is raised, it inherently works to twist or place torque on the supporting frame. A torque box has to resist this without permanently deforming or tipping the truck over. This twisting force is distributed from the torque box through to the outspread jacks. Steel aerials that use separate torque boxes bolted on top of the chassis frame have a higher center of gravity.

The Ladder

Aerial Innovations, American LaFrance, KME, Pierce, and Seagrave fabricate their ladders from

Firefighters in San Bruno, California, demonstrate the strength of their new E-ONE tractor-drawn aerial. San Bruno was the second customer for an E-ONE tiller; the first was Kansas City, Missouri. This is an aluminum ladder with a 500-pound tip load. There is a pre-piped waterway that will extend to the tip of the fly section, but it is shown here pinned back at the base of the fly section.

Two San Bruno firefighters with air packs work at the tip of an E-ONE aerial ladder while it is fully extended at a 0-degree elevation and flows water at 90 degrees to the ladder. This is the position of maximum stress and strain on the ladder. On one side of the ladder is a 500-watt quartz floodlight that provides a work light at night, and on the other side is an electric outlet that powers additional lights or other tools. During extension, the waterway and nozzle slide along the ladder on the bottom of each ladder rail.

welded steel. E-ONE and Sutphen build their ladders from aluminum. Which is better? This question has been asked for as long as the two building materials have been used for aerial ladders—since the 1930s. Depending on who is asked the question, the answers will vary. As for which is best…?

From a manufacturing standpoint, steel is easy to work with and is well understood. Many people are comfortable with steel as it is a heavy structural material. Inherent to steel is a common thickness throughout each piece. Probably the biggest detriment to steel is that it is much more susceptible to corrosion, which means that steel ladders must be painted. The paint not only provides corrosion protection but also offers a surface that is easier to clean. Steel ladders are designed and painted with corrosion in mind; areas susceptible to stress, wear, and abrasion receive extra

protection. Some steel ladders are shot-blasted before painting. Harsher than sand-blasting, this process ensures that any rust, oils, burrs from welding, sludge, and other impurities are removed. Open areas where pieces meet are completely welded to prevent moisture from getting inside to corrode the inner surfaces. Some say that steel holds up better under extreme heat, a condition that can certainly come into play at a fire scene. An additional benefit of a painted steel ladder is that the finish shows discernible indications of exposure to very high temperatures, which may then be given further inspection. Repair work may also be simpler with steel because some feel it is easier to weld than aluminum.

While E-ONE and Sutphen both use aluminum, E-ONE welds their ladders and Sutphen uses Huck bolts (a technical term for a high-strength tension fastener). The fact is that E-ONE and Sutphen vary in their application of aluminum as a matter of design, engineering, and manufacturing decisions. To the extreme that they are both made of aluminum, the inherent properties of both ladders are similar. Aluminum has a higher strength-to-weight ratio than steel. By bolting, Sutphen uses a cold fastening that retains the strength of the aluminum. This is a very precise manufacturing process with extremely tight tolerances. In Sutphen's opinion, aluminum's strength is reduced by as much as half when it is heated enough to weld it. To compensate for this, they contend that welded aluminum ladders require more mass, thereby reducing some of the benefits of using the lighter weight material.

E-ONE uses extruded aluminum, which can be formed in unique shapes. This property allows them to add metal only where it is needed structurally, without having to increase the weight in areas where additional material is not needed.

Contrary to the opinions of some, both steel and aluminum are affected by exposure to extreme heat. Any ladder, after being exposed to significant temperatures, will require hardness testing to ascertain its integrity. Although aluminum's strength can be affected at lower temperatures than steel, more heat is required to raise the temperature of a piece of aluminum than an equivalent piece of steel.

Most aerial ladder failures in the fire service are the result of human error. The collapse of an aerial based on the construction material has not been evident. Which construction material is best for fire service aerial ladders remains a subject of debate.

The Tiller Quint

Traditionally, a tiller, or tractor-drawn aerial, is a basic truck company. This means a crew of firefighters with an apparatus that has a master aerial ladder, at least 115 feet of ground ladders (per NFPA guidelines), plus a minimum of pike poles, forcible entry tools, and, generally, salvage tools and equipment. This differs from an engine company or pumper—known as a triple combination unit—that carries water, a fire pump, supply and attack hose, a minimum of ground ladders, and various other tools and fittings. These two distinct types of apparatus have always had separate duties and places. Beginning in the 1950s and gaining in popularity in the 1960s and 1970s, fire departments began to order aerial trucks with fire pumps, water tanks, and hose. These new apparatus were called quints—short for quintuple combination unit—meaning they satisfied five distinct criteria: they carried water, were equipped with hoses, had the capacity to pump, carried a certain amount of ground ladders, and had a master aerial device—a ladder, or an elevating platform either articulating or telescoping.

Quints became popular with small departments that wanted an additional piece of equipment capable of attacking a fire, and with larger departments hoping to save money by combining an engine and truck to consolidate both manpower and equipment. This concept was carried to a new level with the introduction of the tiller quint. By incorporating a hose bed into the trailer, and adding a mid-ship water pump, a water tank, and preconnected attack lines to the rear of the tractor, fire departments could achieve the strengths of a quint without compromising on the maneuverability of a tiller. With the tank and pump on the tractor, this leaves the full amount of storage space on the trailer unencumbered, except for a small loss for the supply hose bed. The TDA quint can carry all of the equipment placed on a ladder truck and a rescue pumper combined. The fire department in

The tractor for Watsonville, California's, KME tiller quint includes a pump, water tank, preconnected attack lines, and compartment storage for equipment. The tall compartment is shallow in depth because it butts up to the water tank. Below the pump panel is a pull-out shelf for the pump operator to stand on. The bright yellow box at the base of the aerial controls on the turntable is a foot switch where the operator must place his foot during ladder operations.

Encinitas, California, for example, placed an LTI tractor-drawn quint in service that carries all of the necessary equipment for salvage, overhaul, ventilation, swift water rescue, trench and confined-space rescue, cliff rescue, and extrication, in addition to attack lines and supply hose.

Many of the modern companies that build tillers have delivered quints, including Aerial Innovations with Westates, American LaFrance, KME,

LTI, and Seagrave. E-ONE, Pierce, and Sutphen have not yet built any tiller quints. LTI built their first full tiller quints in 1994 for Huntington Beach and Encinitas, California. KME began production of 13 tiller quints for Los Angeles County in 1997, delivered one in 1999 to Pasadena, and another to Monterey Park, California. Seagrave delivered their newest PTO tiller quint in 2000 to Upper Nyack, New York; Westates built a tiller quint with an Aerial Innovations ladder for the University of California Fire Department at the Davis campus in 2000; and American LaFrance's first tiller quint went to Lodi, California, in 2002.

Los Angeles County and City

One reason that the Los Angeles County Fire Department decided to deploy quints was a need to supplement the number of units in the field with fire-suppression capabilities. The modern reality of the fire service is an abundance of emergency medical responses that occupy many engine companies. Having quints allows a fire department to bolster the number of units that are able to respond to fire calls without tying up additional assets. By incorporating the quint into a tractor-drawn aerial, the county did

Los Angeles City firefighters from Task Force 26 secure a fan to a step on their tiller. The opposite side is equipped with another fan and the self-contained breathing apparatus for the tillerman. Unlike other departments that design steps or a ladder at the rear for access to the cab, the LAFD utilizes all available space for equipment storage. LAFD firefighters climb up using grab rails and individual steps that are placed in voids around the mounted equipment and ladders. One such step is visible protruding between the rungs of the wooden ladder with a vertical grab rail above.

73

not have to sacrifice any of the tiller characteristics that they rely on—namely the maneuverability, the multitude of ground ladders, and their standard complement of truck tools and equipment. Los Angeles County tillers carry 203 feet of ground ladders—well in excess of a rear-mount's capabilities—extrication equipment, a generator, and bulk foam, in addition to 300 gallons of water, a 1,500-gallon-per-minute mid-ship pump, and 1,600 feet of various sizes of hose. Some of the quints are outfitted with supplemental equipment for further specialized assignments, such as urban search and rescue. Whereas some departments use a quint to combine an engine and truck, the Los Angeles County Fire Department quints are supplementing the available resources instead of consolidating them.

When the Los Angeles County Fire Department began to take delivery of their KME quints in 1998, they loaned one to the Los Angeles *City* Fire Department (LAFD). The city requested the unit for a six-month evaluation to determine the use of and possible deployment of quints for their department. The county lent the city a new unit, which was rotated between two different task forces for assessment. Task Force 10 in the downtown area evaluated the unit in an environment with heavy traffic, while Task Force 58 tested the quint in a district that included work in the hills. The recommendation of the apparatus committee, based on the field trials, was against making quints a part of the LAFD fleet. One reason was the quint's overall length. The addition of the pump, pre-connects, and water tank extended the length of the tractor sufficiently to render the vehicle more difficult to maneuver. The turning radius for the quint is 12 feet greater than for the tillered units that the LAFD uses, and the overall length is over 4 feet longer. The wheelbase of the tractor is also longer than the wheelbase of the new pumpers that the city is currently buying. Probably the most significant aspect of the negative recommendation is the loss of storage space on the quint. The hose bed on the trailer reduced the ground ladder storage, an important aspect of LAFD fire-ground tactics. The pump and tank added to the tractor meant that the fire department could not carry one of the three large fans that are standard, a rescue cushion, an onboard generator, and a percentage of their typical cribbing. Another factor against the quint is that the LAFD assigns all of their tillers to either a task force or light force. This means that for the city, there is always an engine attached to a tiller. If the tiller needs water, they've got it already under the command of the same captain. The county has aerials assigned without engines as separate truck companies, and, by using quints, they are adding additional water resources without extra vehicles and personnel. This might come into play for the city fire department, though, if monetary considerations require downsizing, whereupon a quint could be used to consolidate a light force into one unit.

The fire department for the University of California campus in Davis (UC Davis) claims to have the biggest and baddest tiller quint west of the Mississippi. Whether or not this is true, they do lay claim to two firsts: They have the first and only tiller quint with an Aerial Innovations ladder and the first (and only as of this book) tiller with a custom tractor by HME of Wyoming, Michigan. Westates of Woodland, California, fabricated the bodywork and the C4T, four-section, 105-foot aerial ladder was built by Aerial Innovations with one pair of H-style outriggers. When the UC Davis department put this unit into service in 2000, it replaced a 1967 Seagrave TDA. Firefighters demonstrate the quint's capabilities here by deploying a handline, a pre-piped master stream from the tractor, and the elevated master stream at the tip of the ladder.

This shot accentuates the long length and large number of compartments that are characteristic of a tractor-drawn trailer. The diamond plate enclosure with the holes houses an onboard generator.

Chapter Four

TILLERS IN ACTION

Not all departments that run tillers use them in the same manner. Most make full use of the abundance of space for carrying equipment and the ability to carry many ground ladders. Others only require the tiller as a piece of maneuverable apparatus and treat it the same as they would any other aerial in terms of what they carry. The tiller quint can be outfitted as a supplemental rig with additional capabilities or can fulfill the duties of multiple companies. Regardless of the way they are deployed, tractor-drawn aerials see front-line service in departments from coast to coast.

Where Are They?

The use of tractor-drawn aerials in the United States is primarily concentrated along the West Coast, with secondary numbers found in service along the East Coast. In between, there is a scattering of tillers to be found in the Plains states and the Midwest. Tillers can be found in Park City, Salt Lake City, and Ogden, Utah, as well as Boise, Idaho. In the Southwest, tillers are used in Albuquerque, New Mexico; San Antonio, Texas; and both Las Vegas and Reno, Nevada. In Arizona, Phoenix operates seven tillers and there are also tillers in Flagstaff, Gila River, and Tempe. Honolulu, Hawaii, operates 8 tillers as part of their fleet of 16 aerials. The larger departments in the Midwest that use tillers are Minneapolis, Minnesota; Louisville, Kentucky; Columbus and Cincinnati, Ohio; Kansas City, Missouri; and Detroit, Michigan. Smaller Midwestern departments use them in Cicero, Evanston, Niles, and Rockford in Illinois; Anderson County and St. Matthews, Kentucky; Little Rock, Arkansas; and Bloomington, Minnesota. The numbers of tractor-drawn aerials are far greater, though, on each of the coasts.

Los Angeles City Task Force 26, shown here, responded to a reported residential structure fire. The Task Force is made up of the aerial, the engine, and the 200-series engine in the back. If the engine is needed to respond elsewhere, the 200-series engine, which is a full triple combination unit, would stay with the aerial and the pair would become a Light Force.

California

California is the largest state in the country and more fire departments use tillers in that state than in any other. At least one TDA can be found in Alameda County, Alhambra, Arcadia, Bakersfield, Belmont (South County), Berkeley, Beverly Hills, Burbank, Chino Valley, Corona, Costa Mesa, Dublin, El Monte, Encinitas (a tiller quint), Fremont, Fullerton, Garden Grove, Gardena, Glendale, Hayward, Huntington Beach (a tiller quint), Lodi (a tiller quint), Long Beach, Los Angeles City, Los Angeles County (using both tiller quints and conventional tillers), Montebello, Monterey Park (a tiller quint), Newport Beach, Oakland, Ontario, Orange, Pasadena (a tiller quint plus conventional tillers), Rancho Cucamonga, Redwood City, Riverside, San Bernardino, San Bruno, San Diego, San Francisco, Santa Barbara County, Santa Clara, Santa Monica, Santa Rosa, Santee, Stockton, Torrance, the University of California at Davis (a tiller quint), Ventura City, Ventura County, Watsonville (a tiller quint), and West Covina. Two of the departments listed, Lodi and Watsonville, added tiller quints, not as replacements, to operations that previously used rear-mounted aerials. Both were able to convey the superior attributes of the tiller to the town administrations and secure the additional personnel required to properly implement these new units. Watsonville, for example, was able to eliminate small supplemental vehicles that carried specialized gear. The vehicles had required additional manpower when the equipment was needed at the scene. In addition, they obtained the ability to carry other rescue equipment that did not fit onto any of their other apparatus but was stored in the fire station, requiring it to be thrown onto a rig when needed, thus wasting valuable time. The two largest fire departments in the country that exclusively deploy tractor-drawn aerials are the cities of Los Angeles and San Francisco. Los Angeles runs 49 ladder companies and San Francisco has 19. Both departments are known for their extensive use of ground ladders, and tillers provide the most ground ladder storage space of any type of aerial.

City of Los Angeles Fire Department

Los Angeles carries 276 feet of ground ladders on their tillers. This complement is made up of extension ladders, wall ladders, and roof ladders. The extension ladders are two 35-footers, one 14-footer, one 12-footer, and a collapsible 10-footer. The wall ladders include two 24-footers, two 20-footers, and two 16-footers. They also carry a 20-foot, 16-foot, and two 12-foot roof ladders. Forty-seven of the aerials are assigned to run as part of a task force and the other two respond as part of a light force. A task force is comprised of the ladder and two triple combination pumpers—one classified as a 100 series, simply referred to as the engine, and the other is a 200-series piece. The units all carry the station number. The engine was formerly called the pumper and the 200-series engine used to be the wagon. The wagon reference dates back to the 1800s when a hose wagon was assigned to respond with a steam pumper because the pumpers had no provisions to carry hose. A task force can have a crew of 9 or 10 firefighters including a captain. In the case of nine firefighters, the wagon has a single operator, the captain along with a driver and the tillerman ride the ladder with one firefighter, and the remaining four firefighters are on the engine. A task force with 10 people would add one more to the ladder. The three rigs generally respond together. If the engine is called to respond without the entire task force, then the 200-series engine and the aerial together become a light force. A light force consists of an aerial and a single engine with a crew of five or six similarly deployed.

In addition to its strict use of tillers, Los Angeles is the largest fire department purchasing wooden ground ladders in the country. One element behind this is tradition: although the LAFD has evaluated

LAFD firefighters from Task Force 27 in Hollywood ascend to the roof of a commercial structure to investigate a reported fire. Firefighters are equipped with self-contained breathing apparatus, axes, and a chain saw in the event that they encounter a fire and have to ventilate the roof.

both fiberglass and aluminum ladders as alternatives, they have decided each time to continue their long-standing use of wood. This practice is common on the West Coast, unlike elsewhere in the country where aluminum ladders are usually preferred. Wood ladders are roughly equivalent in weight to fiberglass but weigh as much as twice that of a comparable aluminum ladder. The single most compelling reason for their continued use in Los Angeles is that wood is non-conductive. Raising or placing a ladder near power lines is but one hazard; the unseen dangers are of even greater concern. A downed power line on the opposite side of a building can charge the

gutters, siding, or other metal trim along a structure where the ladder rests. Sometimes, after a ladder is safely placed, a wire that was previously intact makes contact with it. To avoid both visible and hidden risks of electrocution, the LAFD chooses to use wooden ground ladders.

San Francisco Fire Department

The San Francisco Fire Department also uses wooden ground ladders, which are made in city-owned shops. They have been making their own wooden ladders of Douglas fir and hickory since 1917, based originally on a design by Seagrave.

In San Francisco, a department full of tradition, it is easy to spot firefighters assigned to one of the tractor-drawn hook and ladders. Truckies wear helmets that are painted alternately red and white, as opposed to engine companies' solid black helmets. Here, a firefighter from Truck 5 is the acting officer in charge of the company. A portable flashlight secured to this helmet provides light, while at the same time keeps the firefighter's hands free to carry tools.

While the battalion chief communicates with companies inside the building investigating an alarm, second due companies stand by in the street. Truck crews with their red-and-white-painted helmets carry axes, pry bars, and pike poles. Engine crews have hotel packs of attack hose to carry into the building to use with the standpipe system. Everyone has self-contained breathing apparatus.

Two carpenters work in the ladder shop and the ladders that they build and repair are only for the San Francisco Fire Department. The ladder rungs are turned by hand on a lathe and are made out of hickory or ash. The ladder rails are made of Douglas fir, although they may try switching to hemlock because of the increasing difficulty in obtaining fir of adequate grade. They also make axe handles and castings for the ladder brackets, ladder locks, and pulleys, as well as other castings for spanner wrenches, hydrant valves, shut-off valves, smooth-bore nozzles, wheel chocks, some hose fittings, and the bells and decorative eagles that adorn every front-line engine and truck. The bells are significantly heavier than those that are commercially available. The department uses the services of a local foundry and then completes the items in the fire department shop. Most of the valves they make are named after the individual who designed them.

Although it may seem strange to some that wooden ladders are used at fires, they are strong, rigid, and non-conductive, and are also a long-standing tradition in San Francisco. Make no mistake about it, these wood ladders will scorch and burn when subjected to fire. Yet this fact makes them easy to inspect since burns and cracks are readily visible; the firefighters believe that damage to aluminum is harder to detect. Wood ladders also need to have a strong finish to protect them from the elements of weather and a fire scene. The ladder shop workers spend much of their time refinishing ladders to prolong their useful life.

Most of the trailer has cleared this cone, but a last-minute adjustment is necessary so that the tail doesn't hit. This close-up also shows one of the most time-consuming wooden ladders that the San Francisco ladder shop builds—the 6-foot extension ladder with a pole secured to each of the rails. Leather pouches built right into the ladder secure the 5-foot poles, which join together to make a 10-foot ceiling hook.

Construction of the wooden ground ladders can take anywhere from a day to two weeks of uninterrupted work. On average, the shops spend about an hour per foot for a straight ladder or a week per section of an extension ladder. Some of the shortest ladders are the most time-consuming and labor-intensive to build because they have the most individual parts. One for instance—the 6-foot attic extension ladder—is almost as labor-intensive as the 50-footer. The 6-foot ladder contains leather pouches that are built into each of the side rails to accommodate a 5-foot section of a ceiling hook that, when put together, forms a 10-foot tool. Unlike commercially available ladders, all 17 of the different ladder styles that are made in San Francisco are designed so they can be disassembled for repair.

Like their Los Angeles counterparts, San Francisco firefighters value wood because it does not conduct electricity. This city, perhaps unlike any other in the country, presents high risks to firefighters from overhead electric lines that run very close to buildings and often are found in the very narrow spaces between adjoining buildings. Often these power lines make the use of an aerial ladder nonviable, and firefighters have to maneuver ground ladders in tight spaces with the eminent danger of live overhead wires.

Each San Francisco truck company carries 248 total feet of ground ladders, consisting of one 50-footer, two 35-footers, two 24-footers, one 22-footer, an 18-foot extension ladder, a 12-foot attic extension ladder, a 14-foot roof ladder, and a 14-foot fire escape ladder. The two 14-footers have hooks on the ends for use on peaked roofs and for grabbing onto fire escapes. The three-section, 50-foot ladder requires six firefighters to raise, and the 35-foot ladders require three. The rest of the ladders can be raised with one or two firefighters. In addition to truck tools, each unit carries a hydraulic Hurst extrication tool plus other extrication equipment. The staffing for trucks is a company of five, which includes the

This is a firefighter's view while riding in a rear-facing jump seat in San Francisco. This unit is equipped with an exterior training seat that is visible outside the tiller cab.

driver, officer, tillerman, and two firefighters. All are trained as drivers/operators and as tillermen before they are assigned to a truck company so they can fill in if either operator is not available. Both the driver and tillerman are classified as apparatus operators, which is a position that receives additional pay. Once on the scene of a fire, the officer and firefighters go inside while the driver and tillerman position, move, or set up the aerial as needed. If the aerial device is not going to be used at the scene, then they operate together as a company of five. In the event of a defensive attack at a fire utilizing the aerial as an elevated master stream, the tillerman is assigned to the tip of the ladder to direct the nozzle, while the driver works from the turntable.

In contrast to San Francisco, the neighboring town of San Bruno, California, staffs their TDA with a company of three. Oakland, across the bay, runs seven trucks, all of which are tractor-drawn aerials, each staffed with an officer and three firefighters.

The Pacific Northwest

Several fire departments in the Pacific Northwest also favor tillered aerials, including Kirkland (a tiller quint) and Vancouver (a tiller PTO quint) in Washington. Bellevue, Washington, is another department that uses tractor-drawn aerials—they have three in service. In Seattle, 4 of their 11 truck companies are running tractor-drawn ladders. Seattle is constrained, though, by the size of several fire stations that will not accommodate the long rigs, and must use rear-mounts instead. Portland, Oregon, runs seven of their nine truck companies as tractor-drawns, with the remaining companies being assigned a rear-mount and a Sutphen midship tower ladder. Eugene, Oregon, has a Pierce tiller.

The East Coast

Atlantic City, Camden, Elizabeth, Garfield (a tiller PTO quint), Harrison, Hoboken, Jersey City, Morristown, Mount Holly, Passaic, Paterson, Rutherford, and Trenton are examples of New Jersey departments with tractor-drawn aerials. The North Hudson Regional Fire Department in Bergen County, New Jersey, has three front-line and four reserve tillers from the consolidation of the departments in Guttenberg, North Bergen, Oaklyn,

Truck 2 in Niles, Illinois, is positioned with its ladder to the sixth-floor balcony for an apartment fire in December 1991. The Pirsch tractor-drawn aerial was built in 1970 and has a custom safety cab. This was a four-section, 100-foot Senior aerial with a fixed-tiller cab and manual jacks. Positioned properly as per the manufacturer's specifications, the tractor is jackknifed to the trailer for stability.

Union City, Weehawken, and West New York. Manchester, New Hampshire; Newport and Providence, Rhode Island; New Haven, Connecticut; as well as Fall River, Framingham, Haverhill, New Bedford, Quincy, Salem, Somerville, Waltham, and Worcester in Massachusetts are examples of New England towns with tight streets that always had and will continue to have tractor-drawn aerials for their agility. Both Dover and Wilmington in Delaware also operate tillers. Greensburg, Harrisburg, Monaca, Mount Penn, Paxtonia, Philadelphia, Pottsville, Reading, Shenandoah, Stroudsburg, and Willow Grove are some of the Pennsylvania locations for tillers.

Philadelphia runs 30 tractor-drawn aerials currently as part of a total aerial fleet of 40 truck companies, which includes three Snorkels, two tower ladders, and five rear-mounts. Within the next few years, the rear-mounts will be replaced with tillers bringing the total number to 35, or the entire fleet of aerial ladders. They want to reinstate a full tiller fleet for the ladders because of their maneuverability in addition to standardization of the fleet. Rear-mounts were added in the early 1980s, both because they were less costly and because some of the fire stations were too small for the tillers. Since that time, they have upgraded the buildings and determined that the rear-mounts create a logistical problem during extra-alarm fires when they shift companies around the city to fill in for busy units. Sending a rear-mount to an area served by a tiller does not allow the truck to have full access to the entire response area.

A fire on the ninth floor of a high-rise in downtown Evanston, Illinois, in October 1996 was just beyond the reach of this 105-foot Pierce TDA. The swing-out jacks indicate that this unit was the first generation of Pierce tillers with a Smeal ladder. The truck was positioned in case they would require an elevated master stream to assist with suppression efforts. Sidewalks and parked cars, common obstacles for firefighters, prevented the driver from spotting the aerial closer to the building.

TILLERING

Perhaps one of the highlights of a tiller is . . . tillering. (It may not be a word, but it should be.) Those who have spent time as a tillerman will convey the sheer fun of being able to independently control the rear of one of these enormous rigs. Tillers have been featured on the TV show *Seinfeld*, and in the movies *A View to a Kill*, *Mission Impossible*, and *Evolution*, for one simple reason—because they're fun.

Learning to operate the rear of a tractor-drawn aerial requires a certain amount of skill, patience, and concentration. It's not like driving the front of the truck. For one thing, the tillerman turns the wheel in the opposite direction. When the driver turns the vehicle to the right, the tillerman has to turn to the left so that the rear follows around the turn instead of crashing over the sidewalk or median. Turning the wheel the same direction as the driver would make the truck crab, or travel sideways.

Crabbing, though, is an intentional operation under the proper circumstances. This maneuver allows for precise movements on the fire ground, eliminating the need to jockey the rig forward and backward into the desired location. Intentional crabbing also aids in navigating certain streets filled with parked cars or other obstacles.

Riding as a passenger in a tiller for the first time can be both exciting and nerve-wracking. While riding with the San Francisco Fire Department, I experienced various sensations as the rig weaved through traffic and around corners while responding with lights and siren. Feeling the back of the vehicle moving independently of the front, and coming to grips with the fact that the rear actually had a mind of its own, was fascinating. Upon returning to the station to back into quarters, most

A probationary firefighter in San Francisco sits in the buddy or training seat while an experienced tiller operator shows him how to navigate the training course that has been set up. Without the extra seat, the trainee would not be able to ride along with the instructor and vice versa.

rigs will pull past the bay to line up in a straight position to back in. Not the tiller. As the front heads past the bay or out into the street, the back is already heading straight for the door, ready to maneuver into the station whenever the front catches up.

Optimal tiller performance is achieved with an experienced team of drivers who work together regularly. Headset communication is a necessity today, although the early firefighters did not have this luxury—nor did they have the traffic concerns

A practice course with cones helps to provide training for a novice driver learning how to maneuver the tiller. After making several passes through the test course, the drivers switch positions so the new driver can experience both ends of the unit. This is vital for appreciating all aspects of controlling the unit and understanding how the front, the fifth wheel, and the tiller work both together and against each other.

that are present today. Driving around town and responding to an emergency are totally different. While driving around town, the tillerman simply follows the driver and navigates easy turns. While responding, the driver must occasionally give information to the tillerman about lane changes, abrupt turns, or obstacles that may be in a blind spot. The headset microphones are always open so the driver can speak without having to key a microphone. In traffic, simple statements like "clear" or "watch out" will convey enough to the astute tillerman. Also, "hard left ahead, watch for the red car" might warn the tillerman about an upcoming car that is not yet visible from the rear.

Many drivers act as though they're driving the entire rig—like there's no one at the rear. This minimizes the amount of work for the tillerman because the rear has a tendency to follow the front like a semitrailer. Despite their unique abilities, a tiller can move fastest and brake most effectively when the trailer is in a straight line with the tractor.

The tillerman is constantly watching as if he were in complete control because he has to be able to react instantly. If the tillerman overcompensates around a corner, he could push the rig beyond the point of recovery, causing the rear to fishtail or crash into a stationary object.

If the aerial needs to be deployed, the driver and tillerman have to set the unit in a straight line, or jackknifed, depending on the vintage and brand of the tiller. Communication and training are vital to getting a tiller rig to the fire scene safely and setting it up properly.

FDNY and the State of New York

Along the East Coast, tillers can be found as a small percentage of aerials in New York City and also in Albany, Buffalo, Elmont, Freeport, Glen Cove, Great Neck (Alert Hook, Ladder and Hose Company No. 1), Kingston, Mamaroneck, Nyack, Port Chester, Rye, and Upper Nyack (a tiller PTO quint), New York. Prior to 1964, all 153 of the FDNY aerials were tillers when the first tower ladders went into service. The number of tillers then continued to decline in 1969 with delivery of the first rear-mounts. It is possible that the original intent of the fire department was to replace every tiller with a rear-mount or tower ladder, though this was not possible because of the maneuverability issue in many areas of the five boroughs. Since that time, the number of tillers has fluctuated from roughly 20 in the early 1980s to the current assignment of 12, with further reductions possible. As recently as the summer of 2000, there were 15 tillers in service. If it were possible to do away with the need for tillers entirely in New York City, perhaps

FDNY L-175 runs with a 1994 Seagrave 100-foot tractor-drawn aerial with a fully enclosed tilt-cab. The trailer was designed with large compartments and a full ladder at the rear to gain access to the tiller cab. Stationed in Brooklyn, Ladder 175 is shown here after being special-called to stand by at a construction accident in Times Square.

they would all be removed from front-line duty. New York City has a total aerial fleet of 143 units.

Recent reductions in the number of tillers have occurred for several reasons, including a higher incident of motor vehicle accidents involving tillers when compared to other apparatus. The physical size of firehouses and the rigs has also been a factor. Although the tillers fit into the houses where they're assigned, they are unable to fit into many of the other houses where they are temporarily relocated to cover other districts.

Financial considerations are also a contributing factor in New York as with other departments. The last union contract, for example, gave a 5 percent increase in pay to chauffeurs (vehicle operators) and pump operators in New York. All FDNY ladder companies have an officer and five firefighters, one of which is the chauffeur—tillers have two operators. The cost differential of rear-mounts and tillers is also significant. The most recent figures representing FDNY apparatus purchases put the cost of a rear-mount at $519,479 and a tiller at $645,529—a difference of $126,050 per vehicle.

FDNY tillers are equipped the same as rear-mounts. This means that the additional space for tools and equipment, as well as the larger capacity for ground ladders, is not used to its full advantage. In essence, as stated earlier, the tillers are in FDNY solely to fill the need for maneuverability in the areas to which they are assigned. Of the 12 tillers currently in front-line service, 3 require this type of vehicle due to the nature of the fire station where they are assigned. These are Ladder 35 in West Harlem, Ladder 104 in Williamsburg, and Ladder 118 in Brooklyn. A straight-frame rear-mount would not be able to get into and out of these firehouses. The others are assigned to districts that require the highly maneuverable rigs for the response area. These are Ladder 5 in Greenwich Village, Ladder 6 in Chinatown, Ladder 20 in SOHO (which stands for south of Houston Street), Ladder 39 in the Woodlawn section of the Bronx, Ladder 106 in Greenpoint, and Ladder 143 in the Woodhaven section of Queens. In Brooklyn, Ladder 147 is in Flatbush, Ladder 175 is in Brownsville, and Ladder 101 is in Red Hook.

The Southeast

In Georgia, Fulton County uses one tiller, East Point has three, Gainesville has one, and Orange Beach operates one. Atlanta operates 9 of their 14 truck companies as tillers. Jacksonville, Florida, probably the only fire department in that state using tillers, has four. Birmingham, Alabama, also has a tiller in service. In Tennessee, Nashville has several tillers in their fleet and Memphis has 6 tillers in service out of 22 aerials. Departments in Anne Arundel County, Baltimore City, Baltimore County, District Heights, Frederick County, Hagerstown, Hillside, Mt. Rainer, Montgomery County, Prince George's County, and Waldorf in Maryland use tillers.

Baltimore City

Baltimore City runs 19 truck companies, 16 of which are tillers. They have one Snorkel in service and two conventional rear-mount aerials that are necessary because of size constraints in their fire stations. Otherwise, the likelihood is that all of the aerial ladders in Baltimore City would be 100-foot

Next page: A four-alarm fire at an apartment building in Elk Grove Village, Illinois, required the deployment of several aerial devices. Elk Grove spotted their 1970 tractor-drawn, 100-foot Pirsch Senior aerial to the roof in the rear of the building. This unit was refurbished in 1987 with new bodywork and a Spartan Monarch tractor to replace the original Mack CF tractor. A firefighter's turnout coat hangs on one of the manual stabilizing jacks in the foreground. Another aerial is visible using a pre-piped waterway to deploy an elevated master stream.

tractor-drawn aerials. Baltimore needs the tillers because many older neighborhoods have very narrow streets with tight corners that are usually lined with parked cars. They even deploy tillers in districts that do not specifically require them for maneuverability because of the likelihood that they will be needed to respond to other areas of the city for greater alarm fires. Unlike some departments that use all of the compartment space that the tillers offer above and beyond what is found on a rear-mount, Baltimore does not fill these rigs with any more equipment than they carry on their rear-mounts, with one exception. They have begun to add a compartment of extrication equipment on the tillers that is not on the rear-mounts. In some cases though, they have an abundance of additional space available to them. Baltimore staffs their truck companies with a crew of four. They carry roughly 153 total feet of ground ladders, preferring aluminum to wood largely because aluminum ladders are easier to handle. The longest ladder carried is a 40-footer on the older rigs; otherwise, the newer rigs have nothing over 35 feet.

Baltimore County

In Baltimore County, both career and volunteer stations make up the Baltimore County Fire Department. There are 24 career or paid stations and 33 volunteer stations. Of the paid stations, eight aerials are in service. There is one tower ladder with a platform, and the other seven trucks are all tractor-drawn. None of the six volunteer truck companies run tillers. When the tower ladder in the career station comes due for replacement in two years, the possibility exists that a tiller will go into service in that station. The tillers in Baltimore County are staffed with a crew of four, including the officer, a firefighter, and two drivers who are classified as fire apparatus drivers/operators. Prior to

A tillered aerial is set up and ready to go to work with an elevated master stream. The pre-piped waterway has been charged with three small lines. Pierce built the unit, and the swing-out-style jacks indicate that this is one of the early-generation Pierce TDAs with a Smeal ladder. Telescoping-pole-mounted 500-watt quartz lights on the rear of the cab provide illumination of nighttime fire scenes. The control console on the turntable to the right of the ladder has a large speaker. This is part of an intercom system with the other unit mounted at the tip of the fly section, allowing a firefighter on the ladder to communicate with the operator at the turntable.

RAISING THE 50-FOOTER

Tractor-drawn aerials offer considerably more space for ground ladders than do straight-frame aerials. Fire departments like those in Los Angeles and San Francisco that teach the aggressive use of ground ladders prefer tractor-drawn hook and ladders because of their ability to carry more than the standard complement of ladders. One of the ladders carried on many tractor-drawns is the massive two-section 50-footer. This ladder is rarely carried on conventional trucks for several reasons—one being the infrequent need for its use. This very large ladder is long, bulky, and heavy. If it were stored in the ladder rack of a straight truck, the 50-footer would take the space of several shorter ladders that are used more frequently; storing the 50-footer outside would require eliminating some compartments on the truck body.

Six firefighters are required to deploy the 50-footer in a carefully orchestrated and coordinated process. The two-section ladder uses two long poles—one attached to either side of the base section—to aid the operation. In addition to the six firefighters who position the ladder, an additional person oversees the exercise and calls out synchronized commands during training; otherwise, the company officer will be one of the six on-scene to deploy the ladder and give the directions as they work together.

The process begins with three firefighters on each side of the ladder to pull it from the storage rack. They proceed to carry the ladder to the spot where it will be raised. With the ladder on the ground,

they remove the poles (called stay poles—or, on the East Coast, "tormentors") that are stored along the inside of the ladder and attach them to pivot points on the outsides of the base section. The two firefighters assigned to work the poles will move lengthwise away from the base of the ladder. As the command is given to raise the ladder, two firefighters remain at the bottom to "foot" the ladder—making sure that the bottom does not slide—while the remaining two firefighters lift the ladder from a position roughly a quarter of the way down from the very top. At the same time, the firefighters with the stay poles assist the lifting by pushing on the area that is above the other firefighters' heads.

The first step in raising the big ladder is removing it from the rig. Six firefighters in pairs of two are required to carry the heavy ladder and then raise it. All of the ground ladders used in San Francisco are built by hand in the fire department ladder shop.

With the exact reverse of the procedure used to raise it.

Implementing the 50-footer on the fire ground is equally time-consuming and labor-intensive. Either reason is sufficient in most cases to discourage its use. The 50-footer remains a valuable tool, though, in the event that a ladder of this length is required and an aerial device cannot accomplish the task. It is said that if carrying a 50-footer and effectively using it can save one life, then it is worthwhile to keep it on board.

With the stay poles in place with two firefighters pushing at the top, two other firefighters foot the base of the ladder to keep it from slipping, while the remaining two lift from a predetermined spot and begin to walk it up.

As soon as it is possible, the firefighters at the bottom will help the others pull the ladder to an upright position while still ensuring that the bottom does not slip. The poles are used to steady the top of the ladder, which is now well above everyone's heads. When the ladder is vertical, the poles will continue to steady the ladder as the other firefighters pivot the ladder if necessary to align it with the building. The sockets where the poles attach can swivel and allow the firefighters to move around the ladder with the poles until they are between the ladder and the building. As the ladder is angled toward the building, the four firefighters at the base work to lower the ladder to the building with the help of the poles. Extension, if required, is implemented while the ladder is vertical, before it is lowered to the building.

Once the ladder is in place, the poles are set at a point where they anchor into the ground while the ladder is used. The ladder is lowered

Once the ladder is vertical, the four firefighters at the base work to position it and extend it to the proper length while the other two use stay poles to steady it. The firefighters with the poles pivot around the ladder as it is turned by the other four, always maintaining pressure on the ladder so that it does not lean and fall over.

1999, these units had a company of five. The tillers carry 199 feet of ground ladders and use all of the available compartment space for tools and equipment. In some cases, these trucks are satellite companies for the special teams within the county and carry specialized equipment for confined-space and high-angle rescue or gear for hazardous materials incidents.

Operation of Baltimore County tiller companies at a fire scene calls for the driver to spot the aerial, then deploy the stabilizers, throw the aerial to the roof, and then initiate ventilation of the roof. The officer and firefighter are assigned to forcible entry if needed, followed by an interior search for victims. The tillerman is the outside vent man who is tasked with venting windows in the rear of the dwelling. In the event of a peaked roof that requires a roof ladder in addition to the saw, the outside vent man will put a bit more hustle in his step and then join the driver climbing to the roof.

A 1990 Pierce 105-foot tractor-drawn aerial from Evanston, Illinois, is working at a winter extra-alarm fire in neighboring Skokie. The pre-piped waterway is pinned to the end of the third section. Firefighters working above the nozzle at the tip of the fly section are using their vantage point to monitor the progress being made. They are able to communicate with the firefighter at the turntable via an intercom to relay instructions. The outrigger on the driver's side is sitting between the parked cars along the curb. Deployment of the swing-out-style jacks could have been difficult at this scene if there had been parked cars on both sides of the street, as would have been the case at night.

District of Columbia and Virginia

The District of Columbia Fire Department (DCFD) has traditionally been a big tiller user. From the 1920s until 1983, the DCFD only used tractor-drawn aerials, although until recently, they assigned tillers to only 8 of their 16 truck companies. Recent purchases have brought the number of TDAs up to 13.

In Virginia, tillers can be found in Arlington, Arlington County, Charlottesville, Chesapeake, at the Norfolk Naval Station, Virginia Beach, and in Winchester. The tiller in Charlottesville features a tandem rear axle on the tractor that provides more braking power on the district's steep hills. Norfolk and Chesterfield though recently placed their last tillers in reserve.

Tillers are generally outfitted differently on the two coasts. It is more common to fire departments on the East Coast to have separate rescue companies with specialty rigs for heavy rescue and extrication duties. It is customary on the West Coast to see more of this rescue work combined into the truck company, and a tiller lends itself well to carrying the additional equipment.

INDEX

ALL STEER, 62-65

Aerial Innovation, 22, 43, 52, 68, 68, 75

Ahrens Fox Fire Engine Company, 16

American LaFrance, 10, 16, 23, 28, 32, 51-53, 58, 60-61, 63, 72-73

American LaFrance 500-Series TDAs, 12

Christie (the Front Drive Motor Company), 13

Dash cab, 35, 67

Eagle cab, 52, 53, 58

E-ONE, 49-50, 59, 68-71

Fire departments
    Baltimore City, 31, 42-43, 89-90
    Baltimore County, 50, 91
    Boston, 16
    Chicago, 8, 10-13, 44
    District of Columbia, 29-30, 94
    Evanston, Illinois, 85
    Los Angeles City, 73, 75, 79-80
    Los Angeles County, 75
    Niles, Illinois, 39, 84
    New York City, 19-20, 34, 45, 88
    Philadelphia, 9, 85
    Pittsburgh, 39
    Portland, Oregon, 58, 84
    San Francisco, 11, 80-83
    Seattle, 84
    St. Louis, 45

Fire Rescue International trade show, 50

Freightliner, 51

Full tiller quint, 48

FWD, 18,

Ground ladders,

Grove Manufacturing, 19-20, 26

HME, 22, 63

Hahn Motors, 16, 19, 20-21, 26, 29

Hayes Aerial, 11-12

International Motor Company, 13

KME, 48-49, 60, 63, 68, 72

Ladders
    Wooden, 60, 80, 82-83
    Steel, 70-71
    Aluminum, 41, 68, 58, 60, 68,70-71

Ladder Towers, Inc., 20

Layden, George, 26

LTI, 21, 23, 26, 28-29, 33, 43, 45-46, 48, 50-51, 61, 66-67

Mack, 10, 16, 18, 28

Maxim, 18, 23, 32

MC, 28

National Fire Protection Agency (NFPA), 40, 57, 67, 71

NFPA 1904, 40

Outrigger, 61, 66, 94

Original Equipment Manufacturers (OEMs), 19, 43

Patriot Series, 41, 52

Peter Pirch and Sons. 12

Pierce, 27, 35, 39-40, 47-48, 54, 56-57, 64-67, 72, 84, 85, 91

Pierce Tillers, 85

Pike Pole, 44

Pirsch, 11-13, 16, 18, 20, 23, 26-27, 30-32, 35, 61, 84, 89

Pirsch Tillers, 8, 61, 85 91

PTO quint, 48, 72, 84, 88

Quads, 18

Quantum Cab, 54

Quintuple combination unit, 71

R.K. Aerials, 52

Seagrave, 12-13, 16, 19-21, 23, 27, 34, 38, 41-42, 52-53, 60-61, 66, 72, 75

Simon-LTI, 48-49

Skytop, 32, 35

Smeal, 39, 48, 63, 67

Smeal Ladder, 85, 91

Snorkels, 16

Spartan Motors, 63

Stay poles, 92

Stutz Fire Engine Company, 16

Sutphen, 30, 40-41, 50, 70-72, 84

Tag axle, 63

Thibault, 20

Tiller quint, 53, 72-73, 79

Tillerman's cab (tillercab), 57-61, 86-87, 94

White Motor Company, 13

Ward LaFrance, 21, 26

Warner Swassey, 20

Westates, 22, 72

Author Bio

Larry Shapiro is a photographer whose experience spans more than 25 years. His portfolio includes work for private, commercial, and corporate clients, but his passion lays in his all consuming love of the fire service and all things motorized. During his career, he has provided photographic services for multiple fire truck manufacturers including American LaFrance, Emergency One, HME, LTI, Pierce, Seagrave, and Sutphen, plus truck builders Freightliner, Sterling, and Western Star, in the form of advertisements, calendars, and sales literature.

Larry has provided photography for several books written by others in addition to authoring and illustrating seven books to date. His previous titles with MBI Publishing Company include *Aerial Fire Trucks*, *Cranes in Action*, *Fighting Fire Trucks*, *Pumpers: Workhorse Fire Engines*, *Special Police Vehicles*, and *Tow Trucks in Action*.

Larry lives with his wife and three sons in suburban Chicago where he was born.

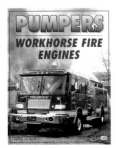

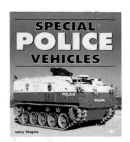

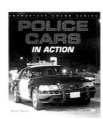

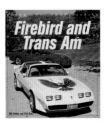